ENJOY THE HIGHS, SURVIVE THE LOWS

A fifty year love affair with football

ENJOY THE HIGHS, SURVIVE THE LOWS

A fifty year love affair with football

Paul Buck

Foreword by Steve Perryman MBE Hon LLD

APEX PUBLISHING LTD

First published in 2016 by
Apex Publishing Ltd
12A St. John's Road, Clacton on Sea, Essex, CO15 4BP, United Kingdom

www.apexpublishing.co.uk

British Library Cataloguing-in-Publication Data
A catalogue record for this book
is available from the British Library

ISBN: 978-1-911476-25-2

Typeset in 12pt Palatino Linotype

Editor: Kim Kimber
Production Manager: Chris Cowlin
Cover Designer: Hannah Blamires

Publisher's Note:
The views and opinions expressed in this publication are those of the authors and are not necessarily those of Apex Publishing Ltd

Contents

ACKNOWLEDGEMENTS

I would like to express my thanks to the following people.

Steve Perryman – Thank you for taking the time to discuss and write the foreword for a supporter who contacted you out of nowhere one day. Speaking to you about this book was as big an honour as watching you lead my beloved Spurs team.

Allen Gittens – A friend and author who gave me invaluable advice, over a couple of pints, when I had completed my book and was unsure of my next step.

Chris Cowlin and all at Apex Publishing – Thank you for turning my dream into reality and making me a published author.

My partner Sarah – Thank you for putting up with non-stop football. I can't help myself and, yes, it is an important match.

Finally, every player I have ever watched, every fan I have ever met, every child I have ever coached and every player that I played with or against. All of you helped form my opinions.

FOREWORD

Bill Nicholson asked in a team meeting early in my career, "Who are the most important people at this club?"

As a newcomer to the first team, I didn't reply in case it was a trick question and hoped that one of the more experienced players would answer.

Nobody answered, so Bill continued. "The most important people at this club are the supporters. They never change. We will all come and go, but they will still be here. They stay with this club. They pay their hard earned money to watch their team and are entitled to their opinion. They are not mugs and if they don't think you are giving everything they will let you know."

In that era, the Spurs fans were regarded as being very critical at times and, over the years, I received my share, but also felt their tremendous support when things were not going our way as they tried to lift us. I will never forget their reaction when Danny Thomas missed his spot kick during the UEFA Cup Final penalty shoot-out. Instead of turning on him, as one, they chanted his name on that walk back to the halfway line. It was exactly what we needed. We were all in it together and went on to win.

At Tottenham I gave my all and the supporters responded to that.

Since leaving the club I am often approached by fans who just want to say thank you for my services to the club they love. It makes me feel proud that they view me in this way.

As a first team player, you can think you are important, but you are no more important than the fan on the terrace, in the seat or in the executive boxes. We all have a role. We will all have different opinions and nobody can criticise them as they are how you personally feel. If you feel it, you feel it.

It hurt when we were relegated in 1977, but the following

season we were lifted by the support from the crowd as we fought to return to the top flight. Thousands of Spurs fans travelled to the away games, including the author of this book. A few years later those supporters could celebrate back to back FA Cup Final victories. The author was there for those too.

When Paul first contacted me about the possibility of writing the foreword, I was a little unsure of how to approach it as I did not know him personally. What I did feel in our conversations was his passion for not just Spurs, but football in general.

The voice of a true supporter is always worth listening to. It is relevant and from a different perspective. It is probably not heard enough. Paul has added to that voice with his book.

Enjoy the Highs, Survive the Lows made great reading for me. With a high Tottenham content, there were many memories and it was fascinating to recall them through the eyes of a fan.

Paul's views on the game are strong and although I do not share all of his opinions, I respect them, as we have viewed them from different angles. He has been there through everything that following a football club can throw at a fan and kept coming back, as fans always do.

I wish Paul every success with this book and am happy to have played my part in writing this foreword for him.

Steve Perryman MBE Hon LLD
- September 2016

INTRODUCTION

Football has always been in my blood. It always will be. From long before I first stood on a terrace it was the most important thing in my life and, to this day, it still holds the same appeal that captivated me as a youngster.

The first time I set foot inside a ground was 1968, when I was taken to see Tottenham play Everton at an impressionable age of seven. After a three goal victory to Spurs, I knew that I was going to spend every possible Saturday afternoon following 'my team'. Now, nearly fifty years later, I feel I am as good a judge as anybody regarding football matters with a host of memories and opinions to back me up.

As a Tottenham fan I have seen all aspects of what can be, at times, a very cruel game, yet at other times put you on the highest of highs. As a football fan I have seen magical moments, players and occasions.

Although my allegiance has been sworn to the Tottenham cause, I have stood to applaud the opposition and give credit when it was due. Not, however, when Arsenal have been the opponents! What I will admit is that the Gooners have played some superb football in recent years, sometimes too good for their own ends.

I have seen my team relegated, and then bounce back immediately. In the early eighties I was present at Wembley seven times in an amazing twelve months when Tottenham's football threatened to conquer all. I have tasted victory in Europe and despair on the same continent. I have seen English sides dominate Europe for years on end and then spend a decade in the wilderness due to non-footballing matters.

From the terraces I have been privileged to watch legends play, Best, Law, Charlton, Moore, Dalglish, Keegan, Shilton, Jennings, Ardiles, Hoddle. The list is truly endless! I have marvelled at being in the ground to see foreign maestros such as Maradona, Cruyff, Platini, Zico, Gullitt, Beckenbauer.

Great managers have come and gone, in my four decades, from the men that built clubs like Nicholson, Busby, Shankley and Revie through Robson and Paisley to Ferguson, Mourinho and Wenger.

I remember the unsung heroes like Gary Mabbutt, one of the bravest players to ever pull on the white shirt of Spurs and, indeed, England. Diagnosed with diabetes, he carved out a distinguished career at the top and is an inspiration to any youngster with ambitions, but maybe held back by some adversity.

Television coverage has changed beyond all my wildest dreams, from an hour of *Match of the Day* or *The Big Match*, we now have every goal, save and incident from every game of any note, almost to the point of saturation. Mind you, how many of us are complaining about that?

Television also brought into my home three tragedies as they happened. I will never forget the feelings that it could have been me and my mates as I watched the horrors of Hillsborough, Heysel and Bradford unfold before my eyes. Nobody should lose their life at a football match and, hopefully, nobody will in the future.

Violence at football matches appears to be pretty much under control these days, but during my time travelling with Tottenham and England it was very much at the forefront of supporters' minds. At close hand I witnessed savage attacks inside and outside many grounds and, on the odd occasion, was unavoidably caught up in the fighting myself. In those darker days the fact that your accent was different was the opening for a fist in the face. Not all away days were like that though, and I have had numerous enjoyable discussions over a pint in pubs close to away grounds with opposing supporters. Never forget football is about opinions and everybody is entitled to one.

Foreign players and, indeed, managers make up a huge part of the Premiership and this can only be good for the fans. On the downside is it good for the national team? The obvious reservation is that young English players will find it harder to break through at the highest level which, in turn, will limit the choice of future England managers to select from. In recent years, Manchester United, Tottenham and West Ham have blooded several youngsters who have made it to the very top, but Chelsea, Liverpool and Arsenal have had virtually none. Indeed, Arsenal do bring through young talent, but not often English! A balance has to be found and it is the duty of the FA to do so. Imports have come a long way since Ossie Ardiles and Ricky Villa pioneered the way for so many more to follow!

The financial side of football has changed beyond anything I could have imagined back in the sixties. Wages paid these days are so far over the top they could be fiction. Premiership stars earning over two hundred grand a week! Can their desire to play on a cold November night be as great as some of the latter day stars who played their hearts out to hold their place in the team? What does the threat of being dropped mean to them when they will still need Securicor to deliver their wages regardless of whether they play or not? Please do not think that I begrudge players earning what they can, I am just looking at it from a fan's viewpoint when some players give the impression of not giving a damn.

In the era of £80 million pound plus players it is difficult to recall the shock of hearing that Brian Clough was to make Trevor Francis the first million pound player back in the late seventies. These days you would be fortunate to get a run of the mill second division full back for that!

Also, for every Roman Abramovich bankrolling his club, there are ten chairmen desperately trying to balance the books to survive. Surely, in the lower divisions it would make sense to go back to a North and South league structure.

Football stadiums have changed beyond compare since that day I first stepped inside and, whilst I was one of many standing on the Shelf side demonstrating at its closure with tears in my eyes, I have to admit White Hart Lane is breath-taking nowadays as so many grounds around the country are. Although I cannot claim to have visited every ground in the country, I have attended matches at over seventy of them. Villa Park, Old Trafford and Elland Road are personal favourites of mine along with Wembley, which is now thankfully open again after a longer than expected rebuilding fiasco.

From having no idea who the chairman of a club was, the men at the helm are as high profile as the players at some clubs. This doesn't always work out and Newcastle are the latest club to be torn apart to the point that the future may be very bleak for the Geordie side.

My team had a bitter boardroom battle which ended up in the high court and the club on the verge of extinction as Messrs Sugar, Venables and, previously, Scholar ripped into each other to gain control. Instead of achieving all their goals they achieved losing the top players at the club and mid-table football for a decade as we recovered.

The England side has been a source of pain in all my time following football. I remember little of 1966, but from 1970 onwards every awful, dreadful, despairing moment has been ingrained in my mind forever!

I have been fortunate to have met many of my heroes off the pitch and that includes the honour of having dinner with the 1966 World Cup team before an England v Germany match back in 1991. To sit with those guys talking football for hours was something I never dreamt I would do, and for weeks afterwards I was walking on air.

I was fortunate to attend several Player of the Season evenings arranged by the Spurs Supporters Club. The players would mingle with the fans and generally just chat about football. Does that still happen today or has the true fan been left behind and replaced by the corporate crowd?

In my earlier years, I would hang around after matches and try to get autographs from the players as they left the ground. I cannot remember anybody saying no and those signatures meant the world to me as a child and still do.

For seventeen years I coached youth football and the feelings I got from passing on some of my knowledge to the next generation of football-loving kids gave me a truly remarkable sense of achievement.

I hope in fifty years' time they have similar memories to mine.

Enjoy the highs, survive the lows!

Paul Buck
- July 2016

CHAPTER 1 – HEROES
My eyes have seen the glory

We all have our heroes. My heroes have always kicked a football.

In this chapter I will look back at the heroes in Tottenham shirts who I have been privileged to have seen and, at the end, try to pick my personal favourite eleven. With dozens of personal heroes to choose from, this could be the chapter that takes the longest to write!

With a history as great as Tottenham's there are so many names to choose from so I have decided to omit any player that was before my time and I did not see. A lot of these would walk into most best-ever teams of supporters older than me, but these legends are out.

Pre-War legends Vivian Woodward and Jimmy Dimmock.

Alf Ramsey and Bill Nicholson from the fifties.

The 1961 Double winners including Danny Blanchflower, Bobby Smith, Cliff Jones, Terry Dyson, John White and Dave Mackay.

I did not see any of them play live so, although I have them in my mind from newsreels and in my heart, they are not included. I have also decided to omit the greatest goalscorer ever in Jimmy Greaves. Although I did see him play live, it was at the very end of his Tottenham career and I did not see him play many times, so most of my memories come again from TV footage.

My first choice of heroes come as a group. The late sixties, early seventies side had some awesome players in it. Pat Jennings, Cyril Knowles, Martin Chivers, Alan Gilzean, Alan Mullery, Martin Peters, Mike England, Joe Kinnear. Most teams will never have eight players as good as this. We had them all at once!

Pat Jennings in goal is quite simply the best I have ever seen at White Hart Lane. People used to say that he had hands like shovels and his sheer size meant it was going to take something special to beat him. His trademark used to be to pluck a cross out of the air with one hand. This wasn't to be flash, as Pat was a quiet gentle giant, it was just natural to him following a childhood of Gaelic football in Ireland. In this era of keepers, not many catch crosses at all and choose to punch everything. Not Pat!

I remember a save he made at home to Newcastle in the seventies which compares to any I have ever seen anywhere. Tommy Craig hit a shot that was travelling like a rocket at our goal. Pat appeared from nowhere to tip the ball over the bar with one hand. I do not recall seeing this on TV since, but it is forever in my memory. Pat made almost 700 appearances for Tottenham. If it were not for those nine seasons down the road, he would surely have passed the thousand mark for us!

Manager Keith Burkinshaw has gone on record saying his selling Pat was his biggest mistake. He is right! It took five years to replace him properly. Pat also made a record number of appearances for Northern Ireland, 119 in total. Many years ago now, I met Pat outside a newsagents in Hertfordshire, where we both lived. His hands WERE as big as shovels!

The defence around this time consisted of the likes of Mike England, Joe Kinnear and Phil Beal. All great players, but my hero was left back Cyril Knowles.

Cyril was a wing back before we had wing backs. His current equivalent would be Ashley Cole or Patrice Evra, forever looking to get forward to support the attack. Tottenham played with so much flair, Cyril was always on the front foot. He was a strong tackler, a great crosser of the ball and struck as sweet a free kick as anybody I have seen since.

Cyril racked up close to 600 games in Tottenham colours, but failed to break through with England playing only four games for his country. His style probably went against him at international level as Alf Ramsey didn't tend to play with wingers at this time, so would never have wanted his full back flying down the wing! Wrong time Cyril!

Cyril became immortalised when a record was released in the early seventies. The Cockrell Chorus released 'Nice One Cyril' in honour of him, and the rapport between player and crowd became even stronger as the song was belted out every match. After retiring through injury, Cyril went into management and brought Torquay and Hartlepool to White Hart Lane for cup ties. Cyril was received like a god.

Sadly, Cyril passed away following a brain tumour in the early nineties. The club held a moving memorial match in his honour in 1991. The attendance was less than 13,000. I was disgusted with Tottenham fans that day for not filling the ground. Shame on you! Cyril deserved one last full house at the Lane.

So when Cyril moved forward who was in front of him? Alan Mullery, my next hero.

Mullers was half man, half tank and would run through a brick wall for the team. Never scared of anybody and full of confidence, he ruled the midfield. For a few seasons there was nobody better in English football, doing what he did. Win the ball, pass the ball! Simple stuff really, but you need the desire to do it. Mullers, as a pundit on Sky Sports in recent years, still has more passion than most current players. He played over 400 games for the club scoring around forty times. I was there for his most important goal. The UEFA Cup Final against Wolves and Mullery had been brought back from a loan spell to help him recover from injury. I can still see the diving header which rocketed into the net to win the Cup! At the end of the game, he lifted the cup in front of the Shelf side, it was the last thing he did in a Tottenham shirt. What a way to go! Mullery played 35 times for England and moved into management with several clubs after hanging up his boots.

My next three heroes, still from the same line up remember, scored almost 500 Tottenham goals between them.

Martin Chivers was everybody's hero not just mine. Big Chiv was idolised at the Lane and he deserved to be.

202 goals in 402 matches. Stunning!

Following in the footsteps of Bobby Smith, Chiv was a man

mountain, but another gentle giant. Recently, I read his autobiography and he says how annoyed Bill Nick used to get with him for not putting himself about a bit more. Chiv proved that he didn't need to. Injuries limited his international appearances to twenty-four, but at club level he was dynamite.

One European night at the Lane against Red Star Belgrade, he came over to take one of his trademark long throws. People talk about Rory Delap these days, but Chivers was doing it nearly forty years ago. Anyway, as he stepped back to throw the ball, he was right in front of me and I patted him on the back. I still recall the smell of Ralgex, or the like, that came from him. Imagine my delight, as a ten-year-old, when watching the highlights on TV that night, there I was patting Big Chiv on the back on TV! At school the next day, I was the hero as my mates had seen that moment also.

Alongside Chivers in attack was Alan Gilzean. Gilly was unique at the time as his heading style was more of a flick than the thrusting header most players adopted. The flicking header Gilly used would send the ball into different directions to normal and give keepers less chance of stopping them. Gilly scored 173 goals in just under 500 games for the club. Another terrific record!

Sadly, Gilly struggled with a drink problem and, since giving up the game, had become a recluse. Some rumours claimed he was sleeping rough and little was heard of him in over thirty years until the club brought him back into some kind of ambassador role.

The third wheel up front was Martin Peters. Martin had already had his finest hour before joining Tottenham having scored in the 1966 World Cup Final. He spent six years at Tottenham averaging one goal every three games over nearly 300 games. Peters took a little while to settle, but when he found his stride, he was majestic, a real class act! He could play up front, off Chivers, or drop into midfield and dictate the pace of a game. Spurs made a mistake letting him leave for pastures new in 1975. His presence was severely missed and Tottenham struggled to replace him properly until a youngster called Hoddle turned up on the scene. More of him soon!

The mid-seventies were a strange and barren time for Tottenham. Billy Nick had stood down after nearly two decades, and the most stunning time in our history, and been replaced by Terry Neill. Coming as an ex Arsenal player, Neill was never completely accepted by the fans,and left after eighteen months, ironically,for Arsenal. Putting an Arsenal man at the helm was always going to be controversial and in fairness to him, the team was struggling as well, which made the job almost impossible. When Neill left the club, we had a real problem. Legends had been replaced with untried kids or third rate players and the club was in a mess, eventually being relegated in 1977.

Heroes were thin on the ground but, with his early steps taken under the management of Billy Nick, a new leader rose. One who would become the club's leading appearance maker, lift trophies as captain and spend over twenty years in the first team.

Stevie Perryman started as a Mullery-type midfielder covering every blade of grass throughout every game. He evolved into a full back and sweeper showing he had a fantastic football brain. On one European night he smashed the ball twice into the AC Milan net to turn the tie in our favour. Why he didn't score more goals was always a mystery to me, as he was always turning up in the opponent's box. The season before we went down, with three games to go we were in a terrible position. A do or die match against Chelsea was an absolute must-win match as they were in the same boat as us. Stevie bulldozed his way into their area to score that day and send Chelsea down instead of us.

Once Tottenham had re-emerged as a force in the eighties, Stevie lifted the FA Cup two years running. He would have lifted the UEFA Cup too, but was suspended from the final. I remember the cruel deflection as he raced back to defend against Real Madrid, which put us out a year later, but all my memories of Stevie are of an absolute warrior who could play a bit too! You do not play almost a thousand games for Tottenham without being a quality player.

Two lesser stars, during the bleak mid-seventies, who have a place in my heart were defender Terry Naylor and flamboyant Alfie Conn. Alfie made less than fifty appearances for the club in three years in London. Injury restricted him, but also his failure to be a team player led to his limited games. At times, you needed one ball for him and another for the other twenty-one players on the field. His long hair and bearded look gave him a rock star look and the crowd loved him. It was no surprise that he ended up being one of only a rare few to play for both clubs in his native Glasgow. For all of his faults, Alfie had superb skill and Tottenham fans had been starved of that for a few seasons at that point.

Terry Naylor spent eleven years at Tottenham making over 350 appearances. I never felt he got the appreciation he deserved as he was a decent player in an average team. Known to the crowd as 'Nutter' he was a favourite at the Lane, he always seemed like the joker in the pack. One game the crowd were singing his name. The next time he got the ball, he stopped running, sat on the ball and waved to the Shelf side. Brilliant for the crowd, but what the manager would be thinking I dread to think!

From the mediocre mid-seventies for Tottenham a true genius arrived from the youth team and stayed in the first team for the next twelve seasons, making almost 600 appearances. Glenn Hoddle was a god at White Hart Lane and would be in every Tottenham supporter's all-time great team.

As I stated in my introduction, I have seen some of the game's greats and, in my opinion, Hoddle is the best I have seen. There was nothing Hod could not do with a football. His skill was plain for all to see, his unstoppable shots a nightmare for any goalkeeper and his passing ability unbelievable. Some people thought Hoddle was a luxury and did not trust the benefits he gave a team. None of those people were Tottenham fans!

I was at White Hart Lane when Hoddle appeared as a sub at home to Norwich. He did okay, but nothing special. On his full debut, away at Stoke, he hit a thirty yarder past Peter Shilton. Hoddle had arrived!

Over the coming years Glenn became the King of White Hart Lane and, as the team improved, there was no stopping him. I will never forget the stunning volleys against Manchester United and Forest, or the solo run against Oxford. The free kicks against Chelsea and Wolves, and the chip at Watford will always be in my memory. One goal I have never seen on TV was a shot against Bolton that flew in from out on the touchline! I was there for all of them and many more. I was fortunate to see such a talent.

Amazingly, Hod only played 53 times for England. Staggering! He was the best player of his generation, but sadly not appreciated by his country. England spent a decade in the wilderness and, in my opinion, pretty much ignored the brightest talent available.

I was at Wembley when Glenn made his debut and scored against Bulgaria with a long range effort. It should have been the start of a century of caps. It would have been if he had been Brazilian, French, Dutch or Argentinian! Sadly, all good things come to an end and clashes with then Spurs manager David Pleat led to his departure to Monaco. The move made him financially secure, but Hoddle should have played for one of the greats of European football like Barcelona or Real Madrid. His talent deserved better!

The eighties brought great times for Tottenham. I have, elsewhere in this book, covered Ossie Ardiles and Ricky Villa's arrival at the Lane. I won't repeat my own words, but will say that Ossie runs close to Hoddle as the best player I have ever seen and Ricky's goals gave me the best night of my life in the FA Cup Final of 1981.

Steve Archibald and Garth Crooks arrived at Tottenham in the same pre-season and quickly gelled into an incredible partnership up front. Over the next few years they struck over 200 goals for the club. Garth had blistering pace and made goals from nothing, Archie got many of his goals from a few feet out. Archie was taken to the fans' hearts, but was sold to Barcelona. Garth moved around a little after leaving Spurs, but suffered with injury and neither player repeated their success at Tottenham.

By this time, Stevie Perryman had moved into defence and was assisted in this department by Graham Roberts, Paul Miller and Chris Hughton. Chrissie was a full back in the same mould as Cyril Knowles and raided down the wing constantly. Robbo and 'Maxie' Miller became the hardest central defence pairing around. Most of their work wasn't pretty, but boy was it effective! Soft centre Tottenham, were no longer a soft touch and these two were as hard as nails. Robbo even played on after Chrissie kicked his front teeth out at Wembley.

If somebody can become a hero and legend in one game, then that person has to be Tony Parks. Tony played less than forty league matches for the club as deputy to Ray Clemence in goal, but played in the 1984 UEFA Cup Final. His exploits in that penalty shoot-out will never be forgotten and he has to be included in this chapter for that night alone.

Clive Allen played for the club for eight seasons, but is included in the main for one amazing season; 1986/87 saw him score an incredible 49 goals as Spurs challenged on all fronts. Sadly, we lost the FA Cup Final, League Cup Semi-Final and finished third in the league. As a team we deserved better, as a player, Clive definitely did!

I have to mention four other players from this era before I move on. Mark Falco spent ten years with the club scoring over 150 goals. At no point did he win the crowd over and I argued on several occasions with fellow supporters who would have loved him if he had played a few years either side of when he did. It was not Mark's fault that Archie and Crooks left, but he was resented by many because they had.

Micky Hazard would have been a legend because he oozed ability. Unfortunately for him, he was around at the same time as Ossie and Hoddle so his appearances were limited to around 200, including his second spell at the club in the nineties.

Richard Gough would have probably become a legend at

Tottenham if he had not been sold after little than a year at the club. Gough was a strong and skilled central defender and I was gutted when Glasgow Rangers tapped him up and stole him from us.

Finally, Terry Yorath will not get many mentions from Spurs fans when heroes are remembered. I remember how important he was to the team when we signed him in 1979. Before he came to Tottenham, Ossie, Hoddle and the rest were getting bullied on the pitch. Terry stopped all that and his presence allowed the rest to play.

The two years he spent with us allowed the team to grow into the team that they did.

The next era saw more legends at the club. Let's start with Gazza!

Gazza didn't waste any time making himself a favourite with the Spurs fans. On his home debut he scored against Arsenal, in his socks. Instant hero! The next five years became the Gazza years with so many highs and a dreadful low. As his game developed under Terry Venables, Gazza became unstoppable. He took games by the scruff of the neck and won some of them almost on his own. Never was this more true than the FA Cup run of 1991.

Gazza was struggling with injury that season, but dragged us past Oxford, Portsmouth, Notts County and Arsenal with some of the best performances I have ever seen from a player. He netted six goals in those matches to ensure a Cup Final day out. Sadly, his career was left in tatters that day with the injury that he never fully recovered from.

As unforgettable and awful as those two tackles he made that day were, I truly believe that a yellow card for the first one would have calmed him down and the second challenge would not have happened. He wouldn't have had a year fighting a career-threatening injury and who knows how great he would have been? Let's remember the brilliance though!

At the same time as Gazza, Tottenham were blessed with

another Geordie capable of being the top man at any club. Chris Waddle struggled to settle in London, but when he did, he really did. Waddle looked slow, but could beat most for pace. He looked lethargic, but could smash a ball from thirty yards past the best. The Waddler had a real purple patch when he started to score classic goals for fun. I remember long range efforts against Southampton and Villa especially. It was a real pity that he left for Marseille just as Gary Lineker arrived. Links hit ninety goals in three seasons, but if Waddle had been providing for him, surely that would have been even more.

Gary Mabbutt spent fourteen seasons at the club making over 700 appearances. He moved from his original midfield role into the defence and became the cornerstone of the club. Many people remember his own goal in the Coventry Cup Final, but not so many remember he had already scored at the other end that day. The fact that Mabbs played at the top for so long with diabetes is a testament to the man. He is an inspirational figure to anybody with such an illness.

Teddy Sheringham was one of the slowest players I can remember seeing at Tottenham, but Teddy didn't need to run! Teddy made the ball do the work and linked the play superbly. He was the complete footballer in my opinion. He could see a pass that others couldn't and could score too. Nearly 150 goals in a Tottenham shirt prove that. Teddy was unlucky that he played in a Spurs team that was in transition as he deserved to win trophies, which he did when he left us.

In recent years, Gareth Bale was amazing. From the youngster who failed to win in his first twenty odd matches to the superstar he now is. He had everything and, since leaving for Madrid, has added heading to his strengths. Lightning pace was always there, but in his last two years with us, he found an end product and hit the net regularly.

Ledley King also deserves high praise. Loved by all of the Spurs fans, he will always be a legend. If he had not been struck with such terrible injuries, he would have been our best centre half ever. In many people's mind, he is anyway. For a player with such bad knees, to not train at all and then stop the best forwards in the land was remarkable.

Finally, two foreigners that are among the best to have played for the club. Jurgen Klinsmann was a World Cup winner when he signed for a Spurs team struggling for consistency. He became part of Ossie's famous five, as our Argentinian boss played five forwards in his formation. The football was out of this world when we had the ball. Without it we were shocking!

Jurgen scored and scored. He was taken to the nation's hearts as he dispelled the negative hype around his arrival and showed that he was an articulate and friendly guy. Unfortunately, one season was all we saw before he went home to Bayern Munich, although he did return for a few months a couple of years later to help head off relegation fears.

David Ginola was with the club for six years, but only played around 150 matches. This was mainly down to managers not understanding him and his talent. If George Graham had been of Tottenham origin instead of Arsenal, he would have played him every chance he had. Ginola was simply breath-taking. On occasions he needed a ball for himself and one for the rest of the team, but what a talent.

Those are my personal legends and players who have given me so much enjoyment over the years. I have been fortunate enough to have met most of them and discussed football with them and always felt comfortable around them.

They say you should not meet your heroes in case you are disappointed. I wasn't!

I have not spoken about Harry Kane or Hugo Lloris as, at the time of writing, their Tottenham careers are still in progress. I have excluded the current crop at White Hart Lane as they are in the early days of their careers at Tottenham.

Walker, Rose, Dembele and co could all be in a heroes' chapter in a few years' time.

So, my hardest task in this book. My personal best Spurs eleven.

I pondered, not for hours, but kept changing the eleven over a few months. I might still change it before the book is completed. How do you leave out some of the names I have spoken about in this chapter?

In goal was easy, Pat Jennings, the best I have seen.

The back four were harder, but in the end I went with Steve Perryman at right back, Cyril Knowles at left back, with Graham Roberts and Gary Mabbutt in the centre.

Glenn Hoddle, Ossie Ardiles, Paul Gascoigne and Chris Waddle make up the midfield.

Up front was really hard to split so many great names. Martin Chivers was a definite but selecting Gary Lineker above the rest was down to my not remembering him miss many chances.

Bill Nicholson would obviously be the manager with Keith Burkinshaw as his assistant. I'm not sure that would work out with two blunt Northerners, but it's never going to happen! Likewise, my eleven is loaded with attacking midfielders. It doesn't matter, they are not going to play any games.

So, with sincere apologies to Ginola, Ricky, Jurgen, Mullers, Ledley and the rest, this is my team.

Jennings, Perryman, Roberts, Mabbutt, Knowles, Hoddle, Ardiles, Gascoigne, Waddle, Chivers, Lineker.

Beat them if you can!

CHAPTER 2 – YOUTH FOOTBALL
The vital part of the future

As I write this chapter, I have recently hung up my boots after seventeen years of being involved in youth football.

During that time I have been privileged to have worked with some wonderful talent and some not so great! I treated each and every one of them the same, always looking to improve the player by looking at the positive rather than the negative.

Too many managers in the youth game are out to earn personal glory by the number of trophies they win and do not bat an eyelid if they replace a long serving player with a better one in their squad. What does that do for the player replaced? Depending on their age or attitude it could be the end of their love of football. Obviously, we all want to be winners, but I have always stuck to my principles and never told any player that they are no longer part of my squad. If somebody chose to leave that was different and they would be replaced.

I have some strong views regarding youth football and know that many people will share them. Why do so many schools not play competitive football? When I first started to help out a teacher at my children's school in Hertfordshire in the early nineties, I was shocked to find out that there was no league and no cups to play for. The only games arranged would be friendlies against local schools and the result was not important. Now it may seem like I have just contradicted myself about the winning being important, but let me explain. I totally believe in competition in life. It starts at school and through your parents. If you give your best and fail, then at least you can be proud that you did your best, but it wasn't enough. That should inspire you to improve so that next time your best will be good enough.

However, if your best is enough that should inspire you to achieve that success again.

Losing, as much as it hurts, is equally important. Without tasting defeat you will never be able to fully appreciate the pleasure that victory brings. Losing respectfully is equally important. I always made a point of congratulating our opponents if we lost and made sure that my teams did also. I have been disgusted by teams that refused to shake our hands after we had beaten them, but told my team that it made our victory sweeter.

With the school team I had little control over selection. My job was to train all ages from Under 7's to Under 11's and make sure it was fun. My personal aim was simple. Get a ball, train with the ball, control, pass, and move. Everything I did was based around the basics. Without control of the ball, youngsters will never be able to improve their game. It is easy to find the big kid and tell him to shoot from anywhere, but if he cannot control the ball, he will be passed by in time as smaller players both grow and develop their skills.

After a while, at school level, we became involved in five and six-a-side tournaments between local schools. The head teacher would give the team a talk before we left and the script was always the same. At first there was never a mention of winning, but a message to 'play the Cranbourne way', and don't tackle too hard! Now I respected her immensely for how she ran her school, but couldn't understand a football team being told that. Anyway, that was soon to change. We won a tournament! Upon our return we were the pride of her school. An appearance on the stage at assembly the next morning followed and future talks before matches involved 'bring the trophy back!' Quite often we did and the head teacher even started to turn up to our matches to lend her support!

As I had now established myself within the school I took control of the non-competitive sports day also. In previous years, every child received a certificate for taking part, win or lose it was the same. The first time I organised the day I made sure the certificates remained, but bought medals for all the winners out of my own pocket. Next step was an inter-house football tournament. Again, I stood the cost of winners medals and also bought a huge trophy for the winning class which was competed for annually thereafter.

During my time training the school team I began an after school football club to which anybody could turn up. It often drew over a hundred kids, most of whom would never play for a team through lack of ability or, in a few cases, a physical handicap, and I was immensely proud of what I was doing for them. As I said previously, we must not shut the door on youngsters that want to play football. We have to keep their interest alive because not everybody will become a player, but everybody can be a supporter.

I would turn up to the school on training days and put up three sets of nets, sort out the cones, balls etc. and even sweep water off the pitch on occasions to enable us to play. I am not special. I only did what so many people across the country do every week. Football lovers give up their time to give something to the youngsters and I have respect for all of them, because without them the game would die.

As much as I enjoyed the school football, I yearned to be involved in 11-a-side football and when my son joined a local side it didn't take long for me to get my wish. I helped out with the training, ran the line and if there was no referee, I would do that as well.

In time, I was invited to take control of the team on occasions and they became more and more frequent, but I was never at ease with the club because they were a huge outfit who would replace players at will. Decent players would be replaced if somebody new turned up who was better. It was not my style and I found it hard to deal with.

After a few years, I moved to the Midlands and that is where I had the best time of my youth football days. I replied to an advert requesting a manager for an Under 11's team called Hundred

Acre, playing in the Lichfield League. I met with the club founder, Colin, and instantly knew this was right. Colin shared the same philosophy as myself on youth football and had started Acre four years earlier to give players that other teams didn't want a chance.

I had six fabulous years with Colin and Acre and enough memories to fill a book on their own. Every season we improved our league position, from fighting relegation to challenging for the title. We made it to three cup finals, but more importantly, we improved the players we had. We kept our squad together and became a big happy family, respected by all our opponents and officials for the way we conducted ourselves.

In Acre's tenth season, and last as the boys were now young men and the following season went into open age football, the squad of sixteen still had nine or ten that had been there from day one. How many teams could say that? It was with huge regret that I was not with them in their last season together, but work commitments had meant that I had moved to Devon and couldn't continue with them. It was with a very heavy heart that I broke the news of my departure to the lads in pre-season training. I knew it would be hard, but didn't expect several seventeen-year-olds and myself to be in tears!

After my final training session the following week, and more tears at the final goodbye, I received a text message from one of the players. Chris had overcome serious health problems when very young and during my time with Acre become a terrific player, more than capable of stepping up to a good standard of football. He had always trained hard, played hard and listened to the advice I had given him. He was also a cheeky lad who loved to give me stick over Tottenham's shortcomings!

His text meant the world to me. It thanked me on behalf of the team for the last six years. All the encouragement I had given them and how I always gave positive advice. He told me that I had become a father figure and role model to him and all his performances in the final season would be in my honour as I had made him the player that he had become.

Nobody has ever said anything to me that has meant as much! People involved with the trophy hunting clubs will never get told something like that.

In my last season, Alex, my goalkeeper in his first season with me, returned to play against his old team, for the first time. Alex had been with them for years and helped them win several honours, but had been replaced as somebody new was deemed to be better. When we arrived he saw his old manager and went to say hello to him. The manager turned his back on him and walked away. People like him should not be involved in youth football, as I told him shortly afterwards. It was disgusting to see, but not unique unfortunately.

Whenever we faced one of our old players, I made a point of going up to them, before and after the match, to have a few words with them. If their parents were there, I would go to them also. Regardless of the different shirt he now wore, he had played for me previously and I would not forget that.

Some of the big clubs in the area used to annoy me. To be honest, I had a real issue with them. Because they were a big club they had a real attitude problem. They felt they had a divine right to victory and in some cases, were unsporting losers who would not shake hands at the end of a match if they had lost.. If they had a player or two unavailable to play, they would call the game off. We would never do that and muddle through with what we had available. It is also a real test for a manager to come up with a solution to a problem. Can Manchester United call the game off if Wayne Rooney gets a cold? Of course not! Why should a youth team be able to? The annoying thing was that the league would allow them to get away with it so as not to rock the boat.

Something that disgusted me one season occurred at the end of a cup quarter-final we played in. After a terrific game the scores were level at 2-2 after extra time. Penalties followed and were all scored until we led 7-6. Then one of the opponents had his spot kick saved by our goalkeeper. As my team raced to celebrate, the unfortunate lad burst into tears only for his manager to berate him from the halfway line! I couldn't believe what I was seeing and consoled the lad myself before having words with his manager.

Another thing that I despise in youth football is the number of cheats. It is a serious problem. Now, I fully understand that, when a parent is running the line, there will be mistakes and I have no problem with a poor decision if it is an honest mistake. What I cannot tolerate is the 'linesman' who will raise his flag every time the ball is played into his team's half. What message does that send out? If you need to cheat to compete, why bother? Who is being cheated? The kids, the reason you are there in the first place! On more than one occasion I had to be pulled away from a cheat after a 'heated exchange'.

Another time I lost my rag was after one of my players had been injured by a vicious over the top tackle. The offending player was sent off, quite rightly, but it was his manager's response which infuriated me. As I carried my player off the pitch, I heard the manager congratulate his player on a great tackle. My player could have had a broken leg and he thought it was great. Another touchline bust up followed and I was delighted to inform him at the final whistle that our 8-1 victory was great!

On the subject of injuries, I must admit to breaking probably every politically correct rule going! In this day and age, a manager is not supposed to touch an injured player as they are a minor and child protection is high on the agenda. I am not a child molester and if one of my players is injured I am going to help him. If that means touching his head, arm, leg, so be it. If he has had the ball smashed in his nuts, he can rub them himself! I have completed a first aid course and have a good idea of the seriousness of an injury. I know how to assess the damage and make the right call, and did on many occasions, including broken bones. The lads were my responsibility during a match and I always said it was like having sixteen adopted kids! I treated them as such!

Parents can be a problem also. I was lucky with Acre as the

parents were fantastic people. Friendly and happy that Colin and myself had their lads' interests at heart and giving the team full support. Other teams were not as lucky with their parents and many feel it is their right to verbally abuse the opposition. You can do that at Anfield or Stamford Bridge, but not in the park! Again, I used to confront anybody that started to give any of my players stick. I would appreciate a good pass or tackle by our opponents and give praise to them, but never cheer a poor effort. Again, what is the point at youth level?

On the bigger picture it is good to see so many clubs setting up football in the community projects these days. For a professional player and coaches to spend time at a school is excellent news. If a Spurs player had turned up when I was a lad it would have been the highlight of my life. For it to be happening these days can only be good for our game in an era when players seem more detached than ever before from the man, or boy, on the street.

There is only so much people like myself can do for the footballing youth. The FA and the clubs have to play their part and, thankfully, seem to be aware of that these days. When players go to clubs for trials they must be made welcome. Many years ago I had players who were treated poorly by clubs upon arrival for trials. Spurs introduced three of my players, not by name, but as trialist one, two and three to their squad. Another club ridiculed one of my players for turning up to train in Spurs shorts! These players were about eleven-years-old at the time and were crushed by the way they were treated. None of them were the same players again. This attitude was probably widespread at the time and, hopefully, the situation has changed as clubs have placed more importance on the youth in recent years.

During my time with Acre I was approached by scouts from Aston Villa, Stoke, Wolves and West Brom. All of them had a good attitude and understanding of how we viewed the situation. I never stood in the way of any of my players and always informed the parents if their son had been mentioned in conversation. I would have loved to see one of my players make it to professional level.

As for myself, am I done with youth football? Only the future will tell me that. I still have the passion and the desire, but seventeen years was a long time. Should I draw a line under that part of my life, finishing on a six-year high with Hundred Acre?

I have fabulous memories.

I have had ex-players of mine that I gave jobs to in the real world.

I have a certificate from the FA for my services to youth football.

I have several team photos hanging in my home.

I had that text from Chris.

I am immensely proud of what I have achieved in youth football and the spirit in which we played. If I have made a difference to any player I have coached then it was all worth it.

CHAPTER 3 – THE FA CUP
Great tradition, but what future?

It is hard to imagine now, but not too many years ago the FA Cup Final was the biggest day in the football calendar.

The final was the only game you could see live on TV all season and was anticipated for weeks before the event. The draw for each round was unmissable, not on TV, but radio at 1 p.m. on the Monday after the previous round had been played. The romance of the cup always shone through as non-league sides frequently upset the odds by beating top flight sides. In short, everybody was up for the cup!

So what has changed?

There are several factors as to why the FA Cup is no longer the pinnacle of the football season. For me, I think the rot began to set in when Manchester United, at the time the cup holders, failed to defend the trophy in the mid-nineties. Pressured by the FA to play a glorified friendly tournament in Brazil, United withdrew from the cup that season. Why on earth they did not field a reserve team at least has always confused me. I get the reason why United made the decision they did; a bucketful of money, but to walk away completely made no sense at all.

From that moment the cup had been devalued and, in my opinion, has never recovered. Top sides began to treat the cup as a second rate competition and picked their sides accordingly. In recent years it has not been unusual for a side to make wholesale changes from their normal line ups using the cup as an opportunity to play fringe players and youth players. The real losers are the fans, especially the ones that turn up to see the likes of Drogba and Lampard, but instead see Mikkel and Kalou.

A few decades ago, there is no way Chelsea would have left

Peter Osgood or Alan Hudson out of a cup tie. This is not a dig at Chelsea, or any other team, just my take on how times have changed. If Chelsea, for example, in recent years began the season with a wish list, the FA Cup would be third behind the Premiership and the Champions League. I understand and agree with that.

I do, however, have a problem when the likes of Wolves or Blackburn turn out eleven reserves. Maybe the answer is for teams competing in Europe to be exempt from the Carling Cup that season and therefore ease the fixture list. After all, the Carling Cup suffers much more than the FA Cup with weakened teams and has sadly, become a real joke of a competition.

The Champions League has undoubtedly had a detrimental effect on the FA Cup. The glamour that the Champions League brings has pushed the FA Cup firmly into the shadows. Until the FA does something to encourage the top clubs to take the cup seriously again, it will stay in the shadows.

Another problem facing the cup today is that foreign imports playing in our league, simply 'don't get it'. In most countries a cup competition is meaningless and treated as such. With so many foreigners in our game, there has to be a connection. The likes of John Terry, Steven Gerrard and Wayne Rooney know the history and importance of the FA Cup while a player from abroad probably views it as a lesser fixture fitted in between the league games.

Managers appear to be the same. Fergie always wanted to win it while you wouldn't be surprised if Wenger put the kids out. It was only after seven years of winning nothing that he started to take it seriously and won it two years running.

TV has to take some of the blame also. As I mentioned earlier, the Cup Final used to be the only live game you could see without going to a ground. From early morning on Cup Final day you were glued to the telly. With loads of interviews with the teams, pundits and fans, a camera on the coach with the team on their way to Wembley and highlights of their matches on the way to the final. It was not to be missed. We even got treated to a Cup Final

It's a Knockout!

Nowadays, with the exception of *It's a Knockout* thankfully, we get most of the rest a dozen times a week. Sky TV has transformed football and I have covered that elsewhere in this book, but the volume and quality they have given us has detracted from the FA Cup Final.

Maybe it's evolution. Maybe I am in the minority that feels 'it was better in my day'. My earliest Cup Final memory was 1967, Tottenham against Chelsea, the first all London final. I remember nothing of the game, although the images are in my head and I have signed prints of Dave Mackay, Jimmy Greaves and Pat Jennings with the cup hanging in my hall. No, my memory of that final is playing with Tottenham balloons that adorned my home that day.

Over the following decade or so, I longed to be at Wembley on this most special of days. Spurs, however, spent this period FA Cup Final free, but my time would come.

I watched as the classic moments happened. Charlie George's strike sealing the double for Arsenal, Sunderland upsetting that great Leeds side, Southampton doing the same to Manchester United, Ipswich and West Ham turning Arsenal over against the odds and Manchester United coming back from two down only to concede to Arsenal in the last minute.

Without looking them up, I can still name the players from any team that played in the Cup Final in the seventies and most of the eighties. They are ingrained in my brain, but I couldn't name Manchester United's starting eleven from last season's final.

I own every FA Cup Final programme going back to the 1950s, but the massive booklets from nowadays conjure up few images. The small programmes of the sixties, seventies and eighties always do. The FA have tried to 'glam up' the competition over the last decade or so, but I feel they have an impossible mountain to climb.

One thing that I, and I believe most fans, hate is the draw for each round, and for a moment, let's put to one side that nobody knows when it is going to be drawn because they keep changing it. It used to be Radio Two, 1 p.m. on the Monday after the previous round. The drama and tension as you heard the balls rattle around in that iconic velvet bag followed by the absolute basic commentary. Number four...West Ham United...will play...number eighteen...Cardiff City. As each home team was pulled out fans held their breath, all thinking either 'that'll do, we'll take them' or 'not us please'. Basic, simple and part of the magic of the cup.

Now we are treated to almost a documentary of the game drawn. Started by Jim Rosenthal, and now adopted by all that have followed, we get...number twelve...Fulham, who played in the final back in 1974 and currently sit ninth in the first division with an unbeaten home record of blah, blah, blah...will play, number twenty...Middlesbrough, who have never won the cup and blah, blah, blah. What a cracking tie that will be at Craven Cottage. Reality check, No it won't! It's Fulham v Middlesbrough, only of interest to Fulham and Middlesbrough fans. Move on!

I hate the draw these days and rarely watch it as I cannot stand the path it has taken. This is the world's oldest cup competition. The final was beamed around the world and Wembley was the ultimate venue. Semi-finals being played at Wembley, in my opinion, detracts from the final. I know the revenue is greater by playing there and more teams and fans get a Wembley trip by doing so, but why not keep Wembley for the ultimate game of the competition only? If it's about the money, play the semi-finals at the Millennium Stadium.

I was at the first semi-final ever to be played at Wembley. Gazza's day against Arsenal which the FA decided only Wembley could host due to the fan base and closeness of both teams to the ground. That made sense to play it there, but set a precedent for all future semi-finals. Looking back, it was another tiny nail in the FA Cup coffin. Playing other league games on the same day as the final has not helped either. If you follow a team to a match that day, you are missing the final. It is as simple as that.

The history of the FA Cup will never go away for my generation, those older than myself, and probably those twenty years younger than me. I know all about the White Horse final of 1923, Bert Trautman playing with a broken neck, The Graf Zepplin flying over the stadium in 1930, Wimbledon's triumph and so many more. I have been so lucky to follow Tottenham to four FA Cup Finals and the replays involved.

Who will ever forget Hereford and the Parka Army beating Newcastle? The commentary that made a career for John Motson. I revelled in delight as York and Wrexham both turned Arsenal over in the eighties and cringed as Spurs were held by Altrincham. Blyth Spartans making the fifth round, Enfield making the fourth and Sutton beating the cup holders, Coventry. Ricky Villa...Say no more!

My love for the FA Cup was awakened recently when my son, who plays in goal for Hoddesdon Town, got to within a round of making the first round proper. I found myself excitedly hunting down times for the draw, something I hadn't done in years. Once they lost, I reverted to the norm and will do so no doubt until something changes.

The drama, romance and history of the FA Cup is in the hands of guardians obsessed with money and image. That is not the best way to move forward.

Can this particular Phoenix rise from the flames?

Time will tell.

CHAPTER 4 – DERBY DAY
The most important day of the season

Unless you have been to a local derby at the highest level, I don't think you can fully understand just how much it means. For weeks before the game you are counting down the days until the match. The weeks become days, the days become hours. Your stomach is tied up in knots and you are caught up in a mixture of excitement and terror!

During the match you feel sick. Depending on what transpires on the pitch you are sent to the highest level of happiness or the lowest depression you can feel. That feeling is with you for days after the match. If you have lost, you start counting down the days until the next meeting. What on earth must it be like to play in one? Knowing that this is the match that matters above all else to all of the fans.

London clubs play several derby games every season. All of them give me a tingle such as I have just described, but with respect to Chelsea and West Ham, Arsenal is the one that really matters. I have no idea how many North London derbies I have been to. I suspect it has to be around fifty or so, yet the feeling has never lessened from the first time.

The first one was a bad one! I was at White Hart Lane in 1971 when Ray Kennedy headed the only goal of the game to not only beat us, but to clinch the league title. On our turf! That was a hard one for a nine-year-old to take!

As the seventies progressed, honours were pretty much shared between the two sides. Visits to Highbury always seemed to see 1-0 wins to the home side with a last gasp winner.

I recall a 2-2 draw one Christmas, when Willie Young tried to fight the entire Arsenal team on his own before being sent off. The intense atmosphere didn't need anything else to heighten the frenzy. Willie was a poor player, but wrote his way into Spurs' fans hearts that day. He erased it when he signed for Arsenal a few years later.

As a Tottenham fan I will never understand how any player can transfer from a club to their local rivals. It is completely unthinkable! I can only recall a few that have moved between Spurs and Arsenal with mixed reactions.

Jimmy Robertson left us at the tail end of his career and David Jenkins came in the other direction. Steve Walford left as a youngster and, as mentioned, Willie Young also went to Highbury. None of these moves caused much of a stir.

Pat Jennings, idolised at Tottenham, found himself being shown the door by Keith Burkinshaw in 1977. The manager believed Pat had seen his best days and young reserve Barry Daines was the one for the future. Daines never really lived up to his promise while Pat had nearly ten more years at the top with Arsenal. Every time Pat played against us for Arsenal he received a standing ovation from both sets of supporters. It is something I never expect to see again. Strangely, Spurs took him back as a reserve in the mid-eighties although he was only used in a Mickey Mouse cup to make up games to cover the European ban at the time.

One player to make the move to find a very different reception on his return is Sol Campbell. In place of the standing ovation that Pat received, Campbell was greeted with thousands of Judas placards being held up in the crowd and a bottle or two being thrown on to the pitch. There was a huge difference between the two moves. Pat was seen as being moved on without wanting to go, but Campbell's move was complicated. With a year left on his contract, Manchester United tabled a bid which was rejected after he said he wanted to stay at the club. At that point Spurs would have received a decent fee and nobody would have blamed him for moving.

A year later almost daily reports indicated he would sign a new contract. When Arsenal first made noises about signing him, he was reported to have said he would never sign for our biggest rivals. But he did! Tottenham lost their captain for no money to that lot down the road. Campbell was slaughtered every time we met Arsenal in the following seasons and also when he came back with Portsmouth. He will never be forgiven.

The worst day I can remember as a Tottenham fan was at White Hart Lane, against Arsenal in 1978, two days before Christmas. This was where our new look Argentinian flavoured side was going to show them. Wrong! 0-5 and the only time I have walked away before the end of a match! Christmas ruined and endless replays of Liam Brady's stunning strike for years to come. A couple of years later we turned them over by the same score, but the lack of TV cameras meant that this famous victory became lost in the memory of the majority.

The FA Cup Semi-Final when Gazza hit that unbelievable free kick past David Seaman is, without doubt, the highlight of all our meetings for myself and many other Tottenham fans. I have a print of that free kick signed by Gazza on my wall at home. It was a day of pure emotion and one of the greatest matches I have ever been to.

The whole season Tottenham had been fighting huge financial problems and needed a good cup run. Gazza that season took us all the way almost single handed. It was such a shame he destroyed his career in the final. More of that elsewhere in this book!

I do not know if the North London derby is the most passionate in English football. It feels like it is to me, but I'm biased. The Merseyside derby was always the friendly one. That has changed in recent years thanks to Rafa Benitez and his disrespectful comments towards 'little club' Everton.

The Manchester derby doesn't seem as intense although the North East derby is quite a lively affair.

The Birmingham derby and the Black Country derby have a fair amount of hatred also. Having lived in the Midlands for a number of years I saw first-hand how much it meant to the fans there.

By all accounts the one to top the lot is the Glasgow derby. Add all of the normal rivalries with religious beliefs and you have a potent mix. Whenever these two meet war is declared. I worked with a Celtic supporter who has promised to take me to an Old Firm derby. I can't wait to savour that atmosphere!

In recent years, I have taken to watching the North London derby in various pubs with a friend who supports Arsenal. We shake hands before and after the game, enjoy a pint or two and for ninety minutes are like aliens to each other.

Every supporter has a match that they want to win above all others. For me it is Arsenal, home, away or on the moon.

CHAPTER 5 – CLUBS
Each to their own

Almost all football fans have their own team they support, but some simply support football. I support Tottenham, obviously, but also appreciate the overall game and other teams. There are teams that I admire, teams that I don't like and teams that I wouldn't watch if they were playing in my back garden. The one thing that they all have in common is that I have an opinion about them, some for the daftest of reasons.

In this chapter I will try to make sense of what has formed those deep-rooted opinions of some of the teams that make up our league.

My hatred of Arsenal and dislike of most London clubs is for pretty obvious reasons, but why do I hate Middlesbrough so much? Why I lean towards Celtic in Scotland and not Rangers is probably a fifty fifty call for many Englishmen, but why do I look out for the results of Livingston?

I'll start in our capital city. My birthplace and where I lived until I was in my early thirties. London.

Hand on heart, I hate Arsenal. I always have done and I always will. I have hurled abuse at their team, their fans and even urinated up the wall of the North Bank at Highbury! I have stood among Italian, Turkish, Leeds and fans of several other clubs cheering against the Gooners at Highbury. Theirs is always the first result I look for after Tottenham's. As our most local of opponents there is always going to be rivalry, but my feelings are deep-rooted for several reasons. As a youngster I remember being told about 'dirty Arsenal' and it stuck with me. They moved on to become 'lucky Arsenal', the masters of the 1-0 win when they had hardly been in their opponents half during the ninety minutes.

For a long period of time, the football they played was boring beyond belief. I cannot say that about them during the Wenger years. Nowadays, Arsenal play with style and skill, sometimes too much to their own cost. Many times, in recent years, I have seen them murder their opponents only to fail to take all the points as their play has involved too much passing and no goals to show for it. In a strange way losing the superb Thierry Henry has helped as they now seem to get the ball in the box a lot quicker which, in turn, creates more opportunities to score. I admire what Arsene Wenger has tried to do in bringing youth through into his first team, but dislike the fact that, Theo Walcott and Jack Wilshire apart, I am struggling to remember the last English youngster to make it at the club.

Arsenal began life in Woolwich, South London. They should have stayed there!

As previously mentioned, the only time I ever left a match before the final whistle was a North London derby, 23rd December, 1978, not that it has stuck in my mind since! Spurs lost at home that day to Arsenal by five goals to nil. I didn't even turn up for our Boxing Day match at QPR even though I had a ticket.

Despite my hatred of the Gooners, I recognise that they are a huge club deserving of their status in the game. They are steeped in history and tradition and, in recent years, have challenged strongly in all competitions.

Currently challenging for everything, but without so much history behind them, are Chelsea. Before the arrival of Roman Abramovich, Chelsea were a bit of a yo yo club that occasionally won a trophy. They might threaten you on the terraces, but seldom on the pitch. Since the Russian billionaire rolled into Stamford Bridge that has changed beyond the wildest dreams of Chelsea fans. Back to back Premiership titles, a Champions League and several cups later, they sit at the summit of English football. Now, I have no axe to grind with Chelsea, and admire the fact that they have had several English players in their ranks throughout their success. I used to love to watch the likes of

Osgood, Hudson and co. in the seventies as they played with flair. That said, there are a few areas that I dislike about present day Chelsea. The fact they are mega rich isn't a problem, but I despise the way they sometimes appeared to buy players to stop other teams from strengthening their own teams. Shaun Wright Phillips is the perfect example. When he was leaving Manchester City, Arsenal looked favourites to sign him until Chelsea threw a ridiculous offer into the ring, ending Arsenal's pursuit. Wright Phillips went to Chelsea where he was behind Cole, Duff and Robben for a place in the team. As a result he hardly played and when he did, looked so out of touch, he was dreadful. It is no surprise that he eventually returned to City where he struggled to get his career back on track.

Another area I dislike is the Chelsea 'plastic fans'. Since the club started to become successful, fans who wouldn't know their way to Stamford Bridge if they were standing in the King's Road, profess to be lifelong supporters. These people make me sick! They used to attach themselves to Liverpool or Manchester United, but see Chelsea as the 'in thing'. This is not aimed at true supporters who were there through thick and thin, they deserve their current glory days. This is aimed at the fair-weather supporter who will lose interest and move on to another club when the tide turns on Chelsea. One of my closest friends is a Chelsea fan who is delighted with their recent success, but remembers the darker times in equal measure. That's how it should be. Football goes in cycles and there are highs and lows, but you stick with your team regardless.

So what happens when Abramovich loses interest and walks away? If he was no longer there, will the club be able to stand the loss of his money? It will be a very testing time for the club when that day comes, so Chelsea fans, enjoy it while it lasts!

The only other London club worth a mention is West Ham. I have always had a lot of respect for the Hammers. They have tried to play football the right way for as long as I can remember. In the eighties, if Tottenham were not playing, I would regularly visit Upton Park. Unlike my visits to Arsenal, I would go with a Hammers fan and stand among the home supporters. The atmosphere was always incredible. The volume of noise generated in that small ground would make even the hardest visitor wary. Even though it was no secret to the fans that I was standing with that I was a Spurs fan, I never felt threatened and was accepted as a football fan. On visits with Tottenham it was different. It would rain coins, bottles and bricks as we left the ground.

West Ham have always produced local talent and, to this day, that is true. In recent years they have struggled to hold on to some of the best young players in the country and been forced to sell Cole, Lampard, Carrick, Ferdinand and Defoe among others. (Where did the money go?) What a team they would have had if they had been able to hold on to them! Hopefully the club will always be able to unearth such talent and continue in the tradition of Moore, Hurst and Peters.

Their long-awaited move into the Olympic Stadium will also be a huge test for them. Can thy replicate that special atmosphere they have at Upton Park? Indeed, how full will the stadium be? I would hate it to end up looking like a game at Monaco where the huge stadium is only a quarter full.

The rest of the London scene is much ado about nothing. In my opinion Fulham, Charlton, QPR, and Palace do not belong in the top flight. None of them inspire me in the slightest and I used to hate visiting their grounds. Millwall, Brentford and Orient belong in the lower leagues, although I have always had a soft spot for Orient. Brisbane Road was the first away ground I visited with Tottenham. I can still remember the nervous excitement of the journey across London on a procession of buses as a schoolboy. Within a few weeks I was on my way to Bolton on my own and the love of following my team around the country was underway. It started at Orient!

Finally, on London's football teams, Watford is not in London! For years it has grated with me as football experts have spoken about them as a London club. Watford is in Hertfordshire. Admittedly, sometimes they would boot the ball so long it might end up in London, but the ground is not.

Also, AFC Wimbledon is the true link to the old Wimbledon. The team were founded when the FA allowed the original club to move sixty miles up the road and be renamed MK Dons. The fans were sold down the river by the club and I hope the MK Dons end up in non-league football. Hopefully, AFC Wimbledon will pass them in the other direction.

Next up...the Midlands. What a sad bunch of underachievers! For eight years, I lived in the West Midlands and have seen just how poor things are. Aston Villa is the only team worth a place in the Premiership. They have it all; history, tradition, fabulous ground, huge fan base and a decent team. I have always enjoyed visiting Villa Park and used to get a buzz just spotting the ground as I passed it on the M6 travelling elsewhere. Villa should, in my opinion, be challenging for the big prizes, but consistently fall short. If Roberto Di Matteo can pull them together and change things that remains to be seen, but they are a club with a host of youngsters who need to claw their way out of the Championship and that won't be easy. If that raw talent can be harnessed in the right direction, and held on to, then who knows what they can achieve?

Birmingham however are not a top flight club. They constantly yo yo between the top two divisions, but are always found out at the top. They are simply not good enough! The club never seems to be on a sound footing and talks of takeover bids are never far away. Their handling of Steve Bruce was shocking when they parted company after he had done so well for them for many years. It was nice to see him keep Wigan up and Birmingham crash out of the Premiership shortly after his departure. Small time club in a big city! The best thing about the club for years was Karen Brady. For a woman to be at the top for over twenty years in a male-dominated sport was a remarkable achievement and I applaud her for that. She has continued to excel at West Ham in recent years.

Black country rivals Wolves and West Brom are a strange couple. Both have histories with bundles of trophies won, but promotions apart, neither have come close to winning a thing in fifty years. Wolves gave me the strangest view of a match back in the early eighties. While replacing the old main stand the club ran out of money. How the work had been started, involved building the new stand behind the old one and then shifting the pitch across towards it as the other three sides of the ground were replaced. When the cash dried up the new stand was open, and the old one demolished, but the pitch was so far away you could hardly see what was happening. I would like to see Wolves return to their former glories and have a team that can compete at the highest level. Unfortunately, I think it is a long way off.

West Brom are another club that are too good for the Championship, but not Premiership standard. I don't see that changing anytime soon. Derby and Forest had their boom times under Brian Clough. What Cloughie did at Forest will almost certainly never be repeated. A nothing club becoming League Champions and then twice European Champions within a couple of years after almost being relegated to Division Three.

The way football has evolved will not allow that to happen again and that has to be a bad thing. Clough brought glory to a small club and lots of silverware too. Forest played with style and were a pleasure to watch. Nobody has been able to follow in his footsteps and, probably, nobody will ever be able to do so!

Derby found the same problem in the seventies. After Clough had worked his magic and delivered a league title to another minor club, they have been unable to compete at the highest level. When they were relegated in 2008, with the lowest points total in Premiership history, it summed up the club. An embarrassment! Week by week it must have been hell for their fans; 4-0, 5-0, 6-0 it got worse and worse. A truer case of fish out of water you will never see! Relegation when it came must have been a relief.

Coventry are in no man's land going nowhere and will not be

top flight material for many years. Leicester had been in free fall since losing Martin O'Neill as their manager, although Nigel Pearson and his team pulled off the great escape in 2015. The incredible title win the following season will go down in history as the biggest shock ever. Claudio Ranieri produced a modern day miracle, but what will follow? I just do not see them staying in their lofty position, but like every football fan, love the fact that they bloodied the big boys' noses.

Stoke are there at the moment, but long ball football teams seldom survive more than a season or two before dropping back down. Mark Hughes has changed their style and they seem to be consolidated now. Time will tell!

Up the M6 to the North West of our country and a real football hotbed. I'm going to skip past Bolton (boring), Burnley (yo yo club), Blackpool (good for a night out) and Blackburn (only on the map because of Jack Walker) for the following reasons.

The four clubs could merge and nobody apart from themselves would notice. They are all stuck in the distant past when they had success, although Burnley could change that if they can stay in the top flight this time around. Sorry, but there are only four teams worth a mention is this area, but what a four; Manchester's City and United, and Merseyside's Everton and Liverpool.

The rivalry between the two cities is notorious, but there are also similarities. Both cities have had to contend with loss. The Munich air disaster and Hillsborough had thirty years between them, but the pain felt was the same. United and Liverpool rose to become what they are today due mainly to two Scotsmen, Busby and Shankley. Eight times European Champions between them, with other European trophies also.

Make no mistake, these four are heavyweights, in every sense of the word, and I respect and admire them all.

Trying to separate them is a bit like asking if you prefer the Beatles or Oasis. Your answer will probably depend on where you come from, so I'll start with Manchester.

United are, arguably, the biggest club in world football and their popularity should not be underestimated. It is alleged that even people in remote African villages, and not speaking English, knew two words of our language. Bobby Charlton! How true that is I have no idea, but United are a global commodity and that is the main reason that they first drew the interest of their American owners. When the Glaziers first took charge there was uproar, but they seem to have left footballing matters to Fergie, Moyes and Van Gaal and kept out of the way. I'm sure they will do the same with Jose.

United have always had a style and swagger about their football. From Best, Law and Charlton to Rooney, Ronaldo and Giggs there have always been superstars at Old Trafford. In between there were such greats as Cantona, Beckham, Robson and Keane. The list could go on forever, but don't forget it hasn't always been non-stop success. As Sir Matt Busby watched his team grow old in the early seventies, and moved upstairs himself, the unthinkable happened and United were relegated. After regrouping under Tommy Docherty, they came back up, but it was almost thirty years before they lifted the league title again. Considering their dominance since then, that is an incredible statistic. Much of it was due to Liverpool's own dominance, but also because United simply were not good enough to sustain a title challenge for years. In cup competitions they were awesome, but not in the league, until the arrival of Sir Alex Ferguson. Even his early years were not plain sailing, but eventually he got it right and all the rest have been paying ever since. Fergie had no problem with blooding youth, and continually did so during his reign. Most of us will remember pundit Alan Hansen announcing to viewers that 'you will never win anything with kids' after an early season defeat. Nine months later those kids had wrapped up the title and several were still there when Europe was again conquered!

I always thought that whoever had to follow Fergie would be taking on an impossible job. I was correct as David Moyes struggled to do so. Louis Van Gaal had the benefit of following

Moyes and not Fergie. Mourinho is following two failures. A much easier ask, although expectations will still be the same.

Old Trafford is one of the best grounds in the country, but a few years ago I was left a bit disappointed after a visit there. I had taken my youth football team to Manchester for a weekend tournament and on the way stopped to take in the ground tour. I was surprised to find certain areas like the boardroom, players' lounge and dressing rooms paled in comparison to White Hart Lane. I expected my breath to be taken away, but left thinking that parts of the interior ground looked like it had been fitted out by MFI. Having said that, the parts that you see on the television, like the pitch and stands are incredible. It was many years since I last travelled to a match at Old Trafford and it had changed immensely.

One final memory on United. They have always had this stigma attached to them about their support not being from Manchester. When I was attending matches there in the eighties, it always amused me that their fans would quite often ignore us and set about their own fans that had travelled from other parts of the country to support them. At least they had some passion then, not like the 'prawn sandwich brigade' famously referred to by Roy Keane.

Across the city, you will find City. A team with the names to match United in the past, like Lee, Bell and Summerbee in the seventies, but since then, almost thirty years of dross and humiliation. Until the Arab money turned up! Since the days when Mercer and Allison took the club to the top they had achieved nothing. A turnstile should have been set up at Maine Road just to keep the constant flow of managers moving! Nobody seemed to be given any time to succeed and, to be fair, not many were capable anyway. Only a supporter of a club whose rivals are successful will truly appreciate how difficult it must be to be a City fan over those last three decades. God knows, much of the last twenty have been torrid for me and my fellow Spurs fans. Everton has been in the shadow of Liverpool for decades also, but

City had to be the longest suffering because of the sheer scale of United's success!

But just as things often have a way of surprising us all, City were taken over and became the richest club in the world. The Arabian zillions that have arrived in Manchester made City a real force again. Post Fergie United became second fiddle to City as countless superstars arrived at the club. Two Premiership titles quickly followed with a bundle of cups, but Europe remains a problem for City and the managerial roundabout continues. Maybe Pep Guardiola will be the answer... Time will tell, but I have my doubts.

About thirty miles away is Merseyside and the other two powerhouses of the North West. Everton are like Manchester City, for so long second best in their own City, but with a rich history to rival anybody. In the early eighties, Everton were once again flying high and among the trophies at home and in Europe. They should have stayed at the top for longer, but parted company with Howard Kendall, the manager who had turned the club around and they have been desperately looking to match his success ever since. David Moyes did well for a few years, but stayed as far away as ever of contesting the title. The Kendall era saw a terrific style of football with names like Gray, Sheedy, Sharpe and Stevens. Lineker followed for a magical season but, since then, their football has been about work rate and not flair. The Joe Royle era earned them the 'dogs of war' nickname and, for me, it sums up the club perfectly.

Across Stanley Park, Liverpool are a different matter entirely! For years the Reds ruled England and Europe. I cheered when they won the European Cup in 1977 and watched their total domination of the domestic game for a decade. Keegan, Dalglish, Souness, McDermott, Rush, Fowler, Barnes and countless others. What a list!

Liverpool played with style. Fans from other teams hated them simply because their own team couldn't compete with them. I went to Anfield in 1978 and saw Spurs passed off the park and beaten by seven. It could have been twenty-seven! They were that good. They not only conquered Europe, they dominated it and would surely have won the European Cup on more occasions if it were not for the ban on English clubs in the eighties. Mind you, it was their own fans' fault that we all got banned, but more about that elsewhere.

After seeing their superiority then, it has been incredible that, suddenly, they completely got it wrong and are now over twenty years past their last title! After Shankly, Paisley, Fagan and Dalglish all delivered the goods, the club kept it in the family with Evans and Souness with limited success. Then they left the famous Anfield boot room and went for a continental approach. Houllier and Benitez have both added to the silverware in the cabinet, but still no league title. Hodgson and Rodgers came and went and Jurgen Klopp is now the man in place. The Supporters would give anything to be the best in England again, but I do not believe they will achieve it in the short term. For several years, Benitez played Steven Gerrard out of position. It took the best part of five years to identify that one of the best players of his generation should not be playing on the wing! A massive problem for me in recent years has been the sheer volume of average players that Liverpool have bought. Suarez apart, there have been dozens of 'average Joes' wearing the famous red shirts. Where are the big names Liverpool used to attract? And don't say Ballotelli!

Liverpool are still a force, but not so much in recent years against the top sides. Fourth, fifth or sixth is about right. The 'this is Anfield' sign in the tunnel no longer roots opponents to the spot like it has done in the past. Surely, it is only a question of time until it does so again!

Eh oop! Into Yorkshire. Another part of the country sadly lacking in top flight football for their established clubs, but, incredibly, Hull City are the current pride of the county. Hull are the only Yorkshire side to play in the Premiership in the last few seasons, but fell back down to the Championship and have just returned. No history and the second sport in their own city behind rugby, what Phil Brown and Steve Bruce achieved has been superb! It remains to be seen if they can stay in the top flight over the next couple of seasons.

Sheffield is home to the Steel City derby between United and Wednesday. With their pathetic record in recent years, they should rename it the scrap metal derby! Nobody outside Sheffield gives a hoot about either of them. In fairness, United were cheated out of the Premiership by the FA and West Ham with the Tevez affair, but they have still not dusted themselves down and got on with things several years down the line. I get the feeling that they will still be bleating about it in fifty years' time, and still in the wilderness.

On the other side of the city, Wednesday are going to be best remembered for a game they never played in. Their ground, Hillsborough, saw almost a hundred fans die in that awful crush during an FA Cup Semi-Final. The club have not done anything on the pitch to make me remember something else about Sheffield.

Finally, in Yorkshire, the biggest club; Leeds United. What has happened there in the last decade is unbelievable! A sign to any top club of how quickly it can go bad if you cock it up big style. For a club to go from ninety minutes away from a Champions League final to the third tier of our football in a few years is unprecedented! From the biggest spenders to being skint has been seen before, but not on the scale that it was at Elland Road.

So where did it all go wrong and who is to blame? Former chairman Peter Ridsdale has taken most of the blame and probably deserves to in all honesty. He was the man who authorised the spending of stupid transfer fees when Leeds were chasing trophies. The squad was added to time after time as he paid record-breaking fees in an attempt to make Leeds United the best once again. As the man holding the purse strings he must have known that the club did not have the money to honour their commitments. That makes it his fault 100%. But in his defence I am going to look at the 'what if argument.

'What if' Leeds had won the Champions League? Millions of

pounds of extra cash would have flooded into the club and the gamble would have paid off.

'What if' Woodgate and Bowyer hadn't beaten up that Asian outside a nightclub? The court case that followed distracted everybody at the club and affected results.

'What if' manager David O'Leary had not spent so much time writing his book, *Leeds United on Trial*, about the woes of the court case and, instead, did the job he was paid to do, win football matches?

All these are factors in what went wrong and Ridsdale should not stand alone as the reason Leeds are in such a mess. I can only sympathise with their supporters who watched as their magnificent squad was sold off at cut price to try to salvage the situation. For a long time it looked like the club could end up going completely belly up and folding. The sale of everything they could sell has at least kept the club alive and, hopefully, one day they will be back in the Premiership, but that could be a long, long time away!

Read the above and don't make the same mistakes Newcastle United! Sorry, you're already hurtling down the self-destruct path.

Into the North East and three clubs who are so different in my eyes!

Newcastle could be heading into exactly the same scenario as Leeds. They have overspent trying to win something, and they have a chairman who has managed to turn the Geordie nation against him. Newcastle is desperate for success. They should have had it under Keegan first time round, but they blew it! Ginola, Ferdinand, Beardsley, Asprilla and co. were everybody's second favourite team. At that time, if Newcastle were on the box, you would watch. You knew you would see fantastic football. They could have won trophies during the Robson reign, but fell short again. Now they are, once again, simply a mess!

The farce over King Kev's second, or was it the twenty-second, departure was sadly not a surprise. Chairman Mike Ashby fools nobody by wearing his barcode football shirt, sitting among the Toon Army. He is only there as a businessman. He will sell to the highest bidder when it suits him to do so. Any manager will have to work with the shackles on and be consistently hung out to dry. So what if the club is in freefall? Not Ashby's problem? If it costs him a few million will it change his lifestyle? No! He will never get the Toon Army on his side, but any fool that thinks that it is a good idea to call St. James Park the Sports Direct Arena; will never care if they are on his side.

Newcastle fans deserve success. They are awesome season after season, but I have one concern about them. For years they could not see past Kevin Keegan. I know he is a hero on Tyneside for what he has done for the club, as both a player and manager, but they have got to move on now! Whoever is their manager must be judged on what he does, not what Keegan has done. Don't forget, as good as it was, Keegan won squat diddly! Maybe one day Alan Shearer will make his mind up and take over at the club. He would have the support of the fans, but will need somebody to guide him as he finds his way. King Kev? You wouldn't bet against it would you?

In the eighties I looked at Newcastle as a feeder club for Spurs. Waddle, Gazza, Ferdinand; their best always seemed to end up at White Hart Lane. At the moment there is nobody at St. James Park I would want to see in a Spurs shirt. That shows how poor they have become. Rafa has his work cut out to pull them back into the Premiership. Personally, and against popular opinion, I don't expect them to bounce straight back up. The core of the club is wrong and needs to be put right first.

Down the road, Sunderland showed signs of finally getting it right a few years ago. Roy Keane as manager was a masterstroke and Niall Quinn as chairman definitely worked. For so long the 1973 FA Cup victory has been the only thing worth remembering about them. Keano could have changed that over the next few years if he had stayed at the club. The man is a winner, I love his honesty in interviews and he assembled a solid squad even if the team was still a little short of first class. Then he left! Then Quinn left! Another half a dozen managers in as many seasons and the Black Cats are fighting relegation annually.

The third club in the North East are Middlesbrough, a club I really do not like. Sorry! My dislike of the club goes back to the seventies and eighties. It always seemed that whenever I travelled to Ayresome Park it was the middle of winter. Freezing cold, raining, almost an entire day on a coach and an awful game at the end of it. Whenever they came to the Lane, it was tedious; 0-0 or 1-0 if we were lucky! Dull, boring football, not what I have been brought up on watching Tottenham. I was delighted when they were to be relegated and, therefore, no longer on our fixture list. I did not miss them at all

The only thing I respect about the club is that they have the best chairman in the league. Steve Gibson has backed his managers financially and, more importantly, with time during his reign. He stays out of the limelight and leaves the football business to his manager. He is a credit to the game. I almost feel guilty for slagging off his club!

It is a pity that the south coast and Anglian clubs have only one representative in the Premiership for many years, but indicates how they have overachieved in the last twenty years or so. Ipswich, under Bobby Robson, deserved to win more than they did. They should have won the title, but kept falling just short. Since then they have had no consistency and are not good enough to be in our top flight. Neither are their neighbours, Norwich, although the Canaries do yo-yo between the Premiership and Championship. Both have nice little grounds and are pleasant to visit. I have been to both on several occasions and, win or lose, had an enjoyable day, obviously better if we won!

Southampton is another place I used to enjoy going to. The Dell was a hole of a ground. Badly designed with a poor view wherever we were put, but they always played good football. Under McMennemy they too excelled and came close to winning the title but, as the years have passed, the club faltered until recently when they have begun to excel again. Under Pochettino and Koeman they have challenged the best, even though their team has been targeted by bigger clubs with big cheque books. Southampton deserve some success before all their stars have flown the nest!

I was at the Dell the day Spurs were promoted back to the old Division One after a season in Division Two. It is one of my best memories, even though for ninety minutes I felt sick with fear that we would mess it up! I danced on the pitch that day.

Portsmouth were the exception to the rule of these clubs. FA Cup winners in 2008, they were at their strongest position since the war. Why did I feel it could all change very quickly? I take no pleasure in being proved correct, but even I did not see the scale of the collapse coming. Harry Redknapp worked wonders for them. He even took a season out to relegate their bitter rivals Southampton for them! Harry knew he had taken them as far as he could and after missing out on the England job and, turning down Newcastle, left for Tottenham. Finances were poor, and players had to be sold. Behind the scenes in the boardroom, things never appeared to be stable either. Relegation followed relegation followed relegation. Pompey went bust and, at one point, they only had around half a dozen players on their books. Trialists and free transfers helped them through those dark days, but it could be fifty years before they find their way back to the top flight.

As I write, there is a classic fairy story going on. Little Bournemouth have been promoted to the Premiership and stayed up in their first season. They have played some magnificent football and deserved their chance. Manager Eddie Howe must be kept if they are to survive over time and they will have to learn that they cannot attack every team or they will get picked off. I hope they survive more than one season. Football needs the romance of a Bournemouth.

Why have we got Welsh teams in our league? We do not have Scottish or Irish teams in our league do we? Swansea, however, play nice football. Very tidy and pass the opposition to death. They are easy on the eye to watch and look like settling into being an established Premiership side over the next few years.

Cardiff are where they belong in the Championship, but have the potential to move in either direction under their owner Vincent Tan. Any owner that is seen booing his own team is not good for our game. Any owner that thinks Cardiff should play in red is an idiot.

With respect to the other teams in Scotland, there are only two teams north of the border, Rangers and Celtic! I prefer Celtic. I don't really know why though! It may be something stupid like I liked their kit when I was young, I cannot remember.

In the last few years, Rangers have had their problems and effectively went out of business, only being allowed to keep the name after dropping Glasgow from the title. Starting at the lowest tier in Scotland, they have risen through the leagues as I write and the Glasgow derby, so desperately needed, is back on the fixture list.

What I do remember is the completely daft reason I look for the results of Livingston! Back in the early seventies I used to buy *Shoot* magazine. Every year at the start of the season they would give away free league ladders. These were pieces of cardboard with slits in them to move team names into their respective positions weekly.

Anyway, the start of one season they printed the wrong team name for a promoted Scottish team and a week later rectified the mistake by printing just one team name; Meadowbank Thistle, later to be renamed Livingston. For some reason, I started to look for their results, possibly I felt sorry for them being excluded by *Shoot* after achieving promotion. I could not name a single player in their history, the name of their ground or even the colour of their kit, but I will always look for their result.

I said it was daft!

CHAPTER 6 – NOW AND THEN
Time changes everything

When I started to go to football matches, Michael Jackson was still black! Spangles were among the bestselling sweets and most homes only had black and white TV sets. Man hadn't been to the moon and only penguins knew where the Falkland Islands were!

A lot has changed since those days. The average man has slowly, but surely, been eased out of being able to afford to go to matches. For many years before I had a season ticket at Tottenham, I would pay at the gate and make my way to where I wanted to stand. Initially, I stood in various places, sometimes changing ends at half-time from the Park Lane end to the Paxton Road end but, in time, the only place for me was the Shelf side. This part of our ground was unique because it was here where the main body of supporters stood, along the side of the pitch. Liverpool had the Kop, United had the Stretford End, Arsenal the North Bank and Chelsea the Shed. Their mass of support was all behind the goal. Only Charlton had a side of terracing similar to us, but they had no supporters to stand on it. I miss the days where I could stand at a match. The match day experience is more like going to the theatre these days until the action starts.

In the first place, just getting a ticket for a top game is almost impossible unless you are willing to take out a second mortgage. If you are fortunate to get past that obstacle, there is no standing area at top flight grounds. I understand the reasons why, but feel that there should be a part of every ground where supporters can stand in safety.

The cost of following your team is one thing, but when you follow them is another. Saturday afternoon, three o' clock everybody played. End of story! Now the match could be

Saturday lunchtime, afternoon, evening, Sunday lunchtime or afternoon or even Monday night!

One Saturday recently, there were three games out of ten Premiership matches that kicked off at 3 p.m. There is no way that I would have been able to have followed Spurs as consistently as I did years ago in this day and age. It would have been impossible! To be fair, in many cases, the grounds back then were pretty rough and the revamp most have had was long overdue. The downside of this, and the removal of terracing, is obviously the cost.

Pitches have improved incredibly over the years also. Many matches used to be played on something resembling a bog, now there is scarcely a blade of grass out of place at the top grounds. Games used to take place if it snowed. Get the orange ball out and scrape away the lines. Crack on! When was the last time you saw that?

There was a time, long ago, when football was a contact sport too. Unfortunately, nobody seems to be allowed to challenge for the ball anymore. If you watch a game from the 70s or 80s on TV through todays eyes, you would be amazed that every game didn't end up three a side. There is nothing wrong in a good strong tackle. I don't want to see players being cut in two, but we have gone too far the other way and contact happens sometimes. Goalkeepers do not deserve a free kick if a forward looks at them from two feet away! They may get touched jumping for a corner.

The balls are lighter. They fly through the air this way and that and boots are now so comfortable that they resemble carpet slippers! Wonder why so many players now suffer broken bones in their feet? Tough one eh?

My last few pairs of boots cost me about £20. Basic Adidas boots. Most of the boys in the youth team I managed wore boots costing over £100! They also had a few pairs each in some cases. Madness!

Shirts were plain with only the club badge on the chest. Now the badge is lost among the logo of an airline, brewery or Japanese computer firm as sponsorship has taken over. I know the money is welcome and a necessary evil, but give me a white shirt with a cockerel on the chest and nothing else any day.

Slowly but surely grounds are being renamed to appease their sponsors. Again I understand it but don't like it. In my eyes Tottenham will always play at White Hart Lane although I am sure that one day the official name will become something like the Pepsi Cola Lane! By the way, Arsenal, the last time I looked, the Emirates was about 5,000 miles away from North London!

Players' wages have become obscene. I do not begrudge them earning what they can, but come on! When I started work in the late seventies, a top flight player was on about double what I earned. Now he will earn in a week what will take me about five years to pick up! I recently saw Viv Anderson being interviewed about winning the league with Forest in 1979 and he said he was on £80 a week back then. Players are no longer in the real world at that level and are the celebrities of today.

My concerns about the changes over the years are simple. If recent trends continue, football will implode. Clubs will spend money they do not have to keep up with other clubs and inevitably some will fold. Players have become mercenary and loyalty to one club is dying out. Players like Nicolas Anelka are examples of the play a season or two and move footballer of today. There are countless others, especially the foreign players, but I do not blame the players. I blame the agents, in most cases, creaming off a large slice of every transfer and taking money out of the game.

My other main concern is that the next generation of football fans will be completely priced out of going to matches and be lost from the sport. There is so much more now to spend time and money on than when I was a teenager. At the risk of sounding like an old fart. It was better in my day!

CHAPTER 7 – EUROPE
Over land and sea

As huge a football fan as I have always been, I admit I watch very little European league football. Sure, I'll watch Real Madrid v Barcelona, the Milan derby and other huge games, but Seville v Tenerife? No thanks! In truth, I find run of the mill European league matches boring. The pace most games are played at sends me reaching for the handset to turn the TV over. Thank the Lord for Sky Sports and their news round-ups from around Europe. Without it, I would be forced to watch more depressing, dull matches!

Despite Inter Milan, Real Madrid and Barcelona having recent success in the Champions League, the Premiership is still stronger and better than the Italian and Spanish leagues. Spanish football is dominated by the giants of Barcelona and Real Madrid with little hope of anybody else breaking the monopoly. Atletico have challenged in recent years, but the sheer financial size of the other two will always hold them off long term. Italy has been dogged by corruption, on and off, for years and Juventus are only just regaining their super status alongside the Milan clubs.

Most of the other European leagues are a procession to the title for the major clubs in those countries. I suppose, to a degree, the same could be said of our own Premiership with dominance from Chelsea and the Manchester clubs in recent years. The difference for me is that there are several contenders in our league, who, with a bit of luck or investment, just might break the stranglehold.

Also, in the Premiership, Palace can beat Chelsea or United can lose to Swansea. Or Leicester can actually go all the way and win it! Our game is more competitive. This has consistently shown over the years in European competition. Over the last decade, Liverpool, Chelsea and Manchester United have not only won the Champions League but, along with Arsenal, contested other finals. It is not unusual to see two, or even three, English teams make it to the last four, and there is no reason why English sides cannot dominate the competition for years to come. How Platini and Blatter must hate that!

A generation ago, England ruled Europe with Liverpool, Forest and Villa winning the European Cup. In the Cup Winners Cup and UEFA Cup, Tottenham, Everton, Arsenal and Manchester United were successful. Another decade before, Chelsea, Newcastle, Leeds, West Ham and both Manchester clubs had lifted silverware on the continent.

How many other countries can boast ten or more different European winners? Without trawling through the history books I would hazard a guess that no other country can match England. Without the European ban imposed on English clubs at the height of our dominance, the haul would have been even greater.

Back to the present and I have a few concerns about European competition and where it is leading. Champions League football has given the big clubs the opportunity to become even bigger and widen the gap, more than ever before, between themselves and their opponents back home. Without exception, Real and Barcelona will qualify every season. The same is true in Italy where both Milan clubs are assured of a place. Bayern in Germany and PSG in France. The competition is loaded with the same names.

How can the Champions League have teams involved that are not Champions in their own country? Humour me here, but my own Tottenham side competed in their first Champions League campaign. Obviously, I was delighted that they did so well, but just assume for a second that they had won the competition. The Champions League winners would be Champions of Europe, but fifty years would have passed since they were Champions of England! Something does not sit right with me here.

The Champions League should be competed for by one team

from each country and the previous season's winners. Like the good old days of the European Cup. The old structure, for me, was much better. The Champions went into the European Cup, the next three or four in the league into the UEFA Cup and the Cup Winners into the Cup Winners Cup.

UEFA, and indeed the major clubs of Europe, will never return to such a solid base of competition for one reason only. Money! The finance generated by the Champions League is phenomenal and, in a world ruled by greed, tradition and common sense have no place.

However, I have a solution which could appease the greed and restore three powerful European competitions.

The Champions League would be for the Champions of each country and the previous season's winners only. To generate the income desired, a league of twenty teams would be formed for that season only. Each club would play each other home and away that season. Each club would be exempt from their national league in that season and return the following season unless they were victorious in Europe.

The teams from each country finishing in the next few places would compete in the same way that the Champions League operates now, in theory. Both of these competitions would create plenty of games and generate even more revenue than the Champions League does now.

The third competition would be a simple Cup Winners Cup as before.

Another plus for UEFA would be that this would, once and for all, fight off the threat of Europe's biggest clubs breaking away and setting up their own league. This has been touted many times over the years and may be the reason that European competitions were revamped in the first place.

Competition on a domestic level would improve also. With some of the title certainties missing for a season, other clubs would have the chance to establish themselves and become more competitive in the future. The downside would be that national leagues would lose the revenue generated by a massive club for a season. This will probably be enough to stop it from ever happening.

Another issue I have with the current format is the way that UEFA make sure that the big clubs stay involved in Europe for as long as possible. Why on earth do the failures from the Champions League group stages get placed into the latter stages of the Europa Cup? It is ludicrous that a team can win a competition that they joined halfway through, and I for one have no interest in the 'competition' at all. I know I am not alone. Champions League football has taken away some of the mystery of European rivals due to the sheer frequency that we meet them.

I was fortunate in the seventies and eighties to see Barcelona, Real Madrid, both Milan clubs, Bayern, Ajax, Feyenoord and the like, at White Hart Lane, but it was the luck of the draw that you met a giant. Now, it is a guarantee that Barcelona will meet an English club, or two, every season due to the format drawn up by UEFA.

There is no disputing just how special European competition is. I hope I have not given the impression that I am against it. I would just change the format. Some of the most magical nights of my life have been European nights at White Hart Lane. I have attended three European finals and celebrated at two of them.

In 1972 Spurs had a first leg lead over Wolves in the UEFA Cup final. Alan Mullery's goal back at the Lane ensured victory. Two years later in the same cup, I saw Mike England keep us level with Feyenoord in the first leg with a 2-2 draw. Sadly, we failed in the away leg and the fans dismantled the ground and the Dutch police force! Ten years on and Tony Parks heroics in a penalty shoot-out meant more UEFA Cup final celebrations.

Without European competition, I would have never been fortunate enough to have seen some of the great players of my lifetime on a pitch in front of me. There is always something special at the Lane on European nights. Always wearing an all-white kit, Tottenham literally shine under the floodlights.

It is in our history, from being the first British side to win a European competition and the way the club embraced the concept, just like Manchester United had done, a couple of years before. Remember, a lot of English clubs were against competing in Europe at its inception.

A previous chapter I have written speaks of managerial pioneers like Busby and Nicholson. They had the foresight to see that there was another challenge away from our own shores. We should all be grateful that they had such vision. We just need to 'tweak' things a little.

CHAPTER 8 – WORLD CUPS
Magic, tears and penalties

The World Cup. The greatest show on earth, or is it?

I feel that over the years some of the shine has rubbed off of the tournament, but am at a loss to know why. Is it just me? Maybe. Could it be that England consistently coming up short has played a part in dampening my enthusiasm? Probably. Time after time, myself and the nation have been caught up with the hype, only to see the team collapse when it mattered most.

Prior to Africa I did not get excited at our prospects for the first time ever. Sure, I had St. George flags adorning my home, but my heart wasn't in it this time. Thank the Lord for that after such an abysmal effort!

Just as likely is the way FIFA have chosen venues for the finals over the last couple of decades. I ask you, America, Korea, and Africa? And now Russia and Qatar to come by 2022. Qatar, in particular, is a joke! A country smaller than London with no football history. A country that will not allow Jews to enter. What happens if Israel qualify? A country where women are treated as second class citizens. A country where the heat in summer will be impossible to play in. I wonder if the fact that it is a country with a bottomless pit of money influenced the decision?

It could be that our own Premier League showcases the world's top players, whereas years ago our chance of seeing the greats was limited to the World Cup. Whatever the reason, I personally need a great World Cup to recapture my interest, especially a great English performance.

Off the top of my head I can still roll off matches, scores and teams from 1966 through to 1990. For me it is all cloudy since then. Obviously there has been the odd highlight, but not like before. Since I was born there have been fourteen World Cups, so here we go with my memories, one at a time.

1962 Chile: I was one, so newsreel tells me Brazil were great and won it, oh and Jimmy Greaves got pissed on by a stray dog!

1966 England: Our finest hour, but all I really remember, personally, is a lot of flag waving and excitement. Again newsreel has given me the full story of England's rise to the top of world football and, like all of us, I have seen 'some people on the pitch' hundreds of times! The players from that team are legends and even if, and it's a bloody big 'if', anybody emulates them in the future, their achievement will never diminish.

I have special memories associated with that World Cup as I have had dinner with the team. I won a competition on Capital Radio in the early nineties and was invited to join the team at the Café Royal in London.

I sat with Martin Peters throughout the dinner and I talked his ears off about his career for hours. Afterwards, he introduced me to the rest of the team individually, with Geoff Hurst remarking on my 'bastard tie'! A few of the German team were also present that evening as well as Terry Venables, Ray Clemence and other current football people of the day. I have several photos of that evening framed in my home and it was one of the highlights of my life.

1970 Mexico: This was the real beginning for me and I watched as many games as I could physically fit in. I had the wallchart, the sticker book, the coin set from Esso.

Brazil were awesome, Pele, Rivelino, Gerson, Tostao, Jarzinho, Carlos Alberto, what a team. Everybody marvelled at this team, so capable of such brilliance, as they brushed the opposition to one side on their way to ultimate victory, never more so than in the final where they took Italy apart.

Pele was the biggest name in the world and this was his stage, skipping past players with ease. I will never forget the shot from his own half that almost found the net, or the outrageous dummy around the keeper. Both of these deserved goals, but even though they both missed they are unforgettable.

England were still a major force and many people fancied back to back glory on the world stage. Even a 1-0 defeat to Brazil in the group didn't dampen the expectancy of a rematch in the final. Nobody told the Germans!

West Germany, as they were then, met us in the quarter-finals and Mullery and Peters gave us a 2-0 lead. England were coasting to the last four until Sir Alf Ramsey took off Bobby Charlton to protect him for the next round. Franz Beckenbauer, the German skipper, found freedom and drove forward for the first time, England tired and slipped to a 3-2 defeat. Stand in keeper Peter Bonnetti shouldered most of the blame for the defeat and the seed was sown for all future World Cups to end badly for England.

1974 West Germany: England, incredibly, failed to qualify from a qualifying group with Wales and Poland! The country was in depression, including the economy, and Sir Alf had been sacked! British interest was on Scottish shoulders, but they fell just short and failed to make it out of their group at the finals even though they played well, holding Brazil to a draw.

This World Cup saw the arrival of Holland and total football. The Dutch were blessed with players that could play in several positions with fabulous skills. Led by Johan Cruyff, the Dutch showed no fear against giants of the game like Brazil and Argentina, beating both on their way to the final against the hosts. Unfortunately, for them, the Germans again came from behind and won the final on their own turf. This Holland team is, in my opinion, the best team not to have won a World Cup.

1978 Argentina: An amazing World Cup! From the stunning spectacle of the home crowd's ticker tape welcome to their teams stunning football the tournament was enthralling.

Once again, England had cocked up the qualifiers and failed to get there! Scotland had made it again, but they cocked it up when they got there! Scotland manager Ally Mcloud and his team left for the finals with a huge send off and claimed they would win the cup. Embarrassment against Peru and Iran, plus a drug scandal, saw their dreams in ruins.

Holland again lit up the competition and, even without the inspirational Cruyff, proceeded to the final. Cruyff had chosen not to travel due to his personal feelings about the military regime in Argentina. His presence might have made the difference.

Argentina had made it to the final also with striker Mario Kempes unstoppable. Indeed, with help from Passarella, Ardiles, Houseman, Luque, Tarantini and the rest, it would have been hard for him to not score! Two more goals from Kempes in the final once again saw the Dutch lose to the host nation in the final for the second time in succession in a 3-1 defeat.

1982 Spain: England were back in the finals after a twelve-year absence and marked their return with a goal after thirty seconds of their opening game against France.

The format of this World Cup had a second group stage which we failed to get through after two draws. Our cause wasn't helped by injuries to key players Kevin Keegan and Trevor Brooking. Both played less than thirty minutes in the entire tournament setting another precedent for future World Cups. Why do we always take injured players? England came home disappointed, but not disgraced.

Northern Ireland had achieved qualification and stunned the world when they beat the hosts Spain. This was the first game I ever watched in a pub, certainly not the last.

West Germany had progressed to another final with the help of a terrible assault by their keeper, Schumacher, in the semi-final against the French when he took out Battiston and avoided being sent off. The French lost their way after that and went out on penalties.

Italy had also made it to the final and, thankfully, with the backing of most of the world beat the Germans. There is normally a stand out player of any World Cup and this one had Paolo Rossi and his goals. For a few weeks he became as unstoppable as Kempes and Jarzinho before him.

1986 Mexico: I have no axe to grind with Mexico, but why did they get two World Cups in sixteen years while we are approaching fifty since our only one?

This was the tournament that saw one man, head and shoulders above all else, almost single-handedly take his team all the way. That man was Diego Maradona. The Argentinian had been kicked out of the previous World Cup as all hatchet men targeted him for special treatment. Finally, he cracked, retaliated, and was sent off. This time he was more mature and set out for revenge. He still took a fearful kicking from opponents, but had the last word with his talent.

Unfortunately for England, we were in his way and he would do anything to win. The quarter-final saw both sides of Maradona, first punching the ball past Peter Shilton into the net, before minutes later taking on half the team to score an incredible second goal. Even when I see those goals now I think, *how did the ref miss the handball?* and *why didn't one of the six players he beat on that run kick the little shit?*

After a slow start England had come good and victories against Poland and Paraguay had taken us to the Argentina game where we were a match for them. Gary Lineker walked off with the golden boot, but it was still a case of what might have been. Maradona deserved his World Cup victory as Argentina duly beat the Germans in the final.

1990 Italy: It is a close call for my favourite World Cup, but this one just edges it over Argentina '78, probably because of England's performance. We should have won this one. We had the team to do it and, ultimately, the chances to make the final. Waiting there was a poor Argentinian team, weaker than four years previously and there for the taking.

In our way was a strong German team in the semi-final, but inspired by the star of the tournament, Gazza, England showed no fear. An unlucky deflection put us behind, but we drew level through Lineker and should have won when Chris Waddle hit the post. The game will always be remembered for Gazza's yellow card and the tears that followed. Minutes later the nation wept as we went out on penalties. England came back home as heroes and for four weeks that summer they had put the smile back on the face of the nation.

The whole tournament was a huge success with the Republic of Ireland also making the latter stages, Italy going well as the hosts, Cameroon's amazing exploits and great football across the board. Unfortunately, the final didn't live up to the rest of the tournament and Germany beat the Argies in a bad-tempered match.

1994 USA: Even now I do not believe America got to host the World Cup! The poorest World Cup I can remember, once again without England. Memorable for the opening and end, seeing missed penalties by people with tight curly perms! Diana Ross fluffed hers in the opening ceremony while Roberto Baggio's cost Italy the trophy in the final against Brazil!

1998 France: Once again it was a case of what might have been for England. Progressing through the group we faced Argentina in the knockout stages. Coming from a goal down, England took the lead through Michael Owen's wonder goal before a young David Beckham's petulant kick saw him sent off and our chances weakened. Incredibly, the ten men 'scored' a winning goal only for the ref to wrongly rule it out and then watched Ince and Batty cock up their spot kicks in the shoot-out. Once again, we had grasped defeat from the clutches of victory!

The French impressed all through the tournament and deservedly took the trophy thumping Brazil in the final. The Brazilian Ronaldo was the centre of one of the strangest stories in World Cup history before the final. To this day, I don't think the truth has come out about what occurred in the changing room before the final. Did he have a fit? Was he forced to play by Nike? All we can really know for sure is that he was not the player we all knew he was that night!

2002 Japan and South Korea: Okay, I get why the tournament was hosted in Asia. Money, money, money! Thousands of shirts sold and ongoing investment, but something is missing for me when the World Cup goes to a non-traditional location.

England went to the finals with the golden generation of players. These guys were destined for glory, we were all informed. Why then did we cock it up again? We also had a foreign manager at the helm in Sven. Nice enough bloke, likes the ladies and is always immaculate in his appearance, but tactically hopeless! If Plan A doesn't work there was absolutely no Plan B!

A quarter-final defeat to Brazil on paper sounds respectable, but not from being in front against ten men! Why did we not go for the kill, instead retreating twenty yards and letting Brazil back into a game they had no right to win? It didn't help that David Seaman got caught out by a long range fluke by Ronaldinho either! Am I the only person that always saw that fault in his game? Add to Ronaldinho, Gazza, Koeman, Nayim, Hamann and some Macedonian just off the top of my head. They all have beaten Seaman from miles out in important games!

Apart from the fanatical Asian support, backing anybody that was playing, the stand out moment for me that summer was Rivaldo's hilarious face clutching after the ball had hit his knee! Brilliant player, poor actor!

2006 Germany: Sven was still at the helm and managed to mess it up before we got on the bloody plane this time! His inclusion of Theo Walcott was ridiculous. Why take somebody that had never kicked a ball in top flight football? And if you do take him, then why not play him? Maybe it was past his bedtime? Anyway, the same old story unravelled in front of our eyes. Lose on penalties (to Portugal), star man sent off (Rooney), obligatory injured player we persevere with (Beckham).

The competition itself has left little impression on my memory other than Zidane losing his mind with that head butt in the final. What a way to finish your career, but sadly for such a brilliant player, the thing that everybody remembers about him to this day!

2010 South Africa: Where to start? Surely the worst ever English performance at a World Cup! Draws against the USA and Algeria followed by victory against the giants of Slovenia saw us, rather fortunately, progress to face the Germans. An absolute humbling followed and you can bellyache about Lampard's goal that never was as much as you want, but we were totally outclassed that day.

So what went wrong? Fabio Capello failed to be true to his word by taking injured and out of form players and it cost us dear. Rooney just did not turn up and should have been given the kick up the bum he needed by being dropped. The goalkeeping situation was a joke with three keepers flying out and not knowing who was the number one. Then he picks Rob Green who gets beat by the softest shot ever and gets dropped.

The squad as a whole looked miserable and, at times, disinterested. I do not buy into the tiredness excuse and never will. There was obvious disharmony in the camp and John Terry's comments were from the heart when he said it is time to stand up if anybody wasn't happy. The fact he was hung out to dry by the rest of the squad speaks volumes about the unity in the camp. Was that a bit of payback for knocking off Wayne Bridge's bird?

Also, what was Capello doing bringing Jamie Carragher back? It was Carragher's choice to quit England so he should have never got anywhere near an opportunity for a month at the World Cup. Same goes for Paul Scholes, great player that he has been, but he quit his country, why beg him to come back? What message does that send out to players on the fringe?

So there we are, needing a goal. Who do we send on? Emile Heskey! For the love of God! What must Peter Crouch have been thinking? By no means the best striker around, but always seems to score for England. Heskey, in comparison, would struggle to score in a brothel!

Away from England's depressing tournament there wasn't too much to shout about anywhere. Even if you did shout nobody would have heard you above those awful vuvuzelas! Another low was the fact that the tournament was played with a beach ball. Why change to a ball that even Lionel Messi struggled to control? Madness!

In a tournament where the big names all failed to light up the stage, I genuinely fancied the Dutch as they were playing as a team. Unfortunately for them, they got to the final and decided to kick Spain off the park instead of playing football and got beat.

2014 Brazil: I hoped the fact the tournament was being held in a proper football country would bring out the best in football's elite. In my opinion, it didn't.

Defeats to Uruguay and Italy meant England returned home quicker than ever before. Manager Roy Hodgson failed to resign as he should have done and lasted another two years until Iceland finished him off in the Euros. Iceland! Bloody hell!

Brazil crumbled under the weight of expectancy from the home supporters and conceded seven to eventual winners Germany.

Which takes us to the next World Cup, to be held in 2018 in Russia.

I hope England have an English manager capable of changing things and being decisive.

I hope we do not take any injured players with us.

I hope we do not go to penalties.

Above all else, I hope I will look back in the future and say, "What a great World Cup that was!"

CHAPTER 9 – PLAYING DAYS
The happiest of times

Welcome to the shortest chapter in the book…my playing days! As I am in charge of the keypad I can put a host of great achievements here, but I won't succumb to temptation and will stick to the facts.

I could write that I was never discovered or that I wasn't given a chance, but the truth is I wasn't good enough! True, if I had pushed things a bit harder, I may have played at a better level, but I was happy enough with my team, packed full of mates and, in truth, didn't expect it to end through injury when I was twenty-two.

At school, I played my first competitive football for Eldon Road Juniors, aged about eleven. I can remember the shock when my name was called out in assembly to represent the school, as at the trial the previous day I had been asked to play in goal as the first choice keeper was sick. From my performance between the sticks the sports teacher picked me for the right side of midfield! The obvious wealth of knowledge this soccer supremo brought to the school was in more evidence before kick-off. When I asked him my role in the side, meaning was I defensive or attacking, I was told to 'run around a bit'. So headless chicken it was then, as I covered myself in something far removed from glory!

I honestly cannot remember a great deal about any of the matches as we never made it anywhere in the cups and were always mid-table in a league of about sixteen schools. Those were the days when schools could compete with each other, not like the nanny state situation most areas adopt these days with no official competitive matches.

Strangely, the one thing I do remember vividly is the

embarrassment I felt when, upon turning up for school one day, I was informed that the school team photo was to be taken that day. No horror there you might think, but I didn't know in advance and had no kit. After frantically asking everybody in sight I managed to get a shirt, shorts and trainers. Problem solved? No! Soccer supremo struck again and placed me on the end of the line with ankle socks in full view. I still have the photo and all these years later I'm glad I didn't rip it up in disgust.

Whilst at junior school I was on the winning side of the inter-house tournament, memorable for two things. My first competitive goal, in the final no less, and the fact that we beat a class a year older than ourselves in the same game. Not the smartest move, but the winner's medal was worth being chased around the playground for the next few days!

Senior school saw little competitive football as two schools merged at that age and my opposition for a place doubled. At this age I had evolved into a strong cross country runner and was always head to head with a mate called Steve vying to be the best in the school. Honours were equal overall and nobody else could get near us. We both represented the school in the Borough Championships and I went on to also represent the Borough on several occasions.

The next taste of playing in a team came when I was sixteen. I was working in a printers, earning decent money and had discovered the pub! Now this pub didn't take a lot of discovering as it was only a couple of minutes' walk from home, but to make sure I was certain of the route I went there every night! 'The pub became the centre of our universe as it had everything we needed; pool tables, dartboards, jukebox and beer! All nights began or ended there and I quickly found a new talent. I was mustard on the pool tables! I was nicknamed 'The King' by our resident bookie and won as much in backing my ability as I was earning as an apprentice printer. I soon grew in confidence enough to go to other pubs and hustle the locals and, thinking back, have no idea how I survived doing that in some of the dives I went to!

Anyway, back to the football. I had just made it back to the pub in time for last orders after following Spurs somewhere one Saturday when the call from another soccer supremo came.

"Oy, Paul, you got any football boots?"

"Yeah, why?"

"Be outside for nine in the morning, you're in the team!"

With the extensive negotiations over I was signed up for Edmonton Green F.C. the team based at the pub and playing in the Brooke Waltham and District Sunday League in North London.

Nine o'clock the following morning I realised just what I had signed up to. Knowing almost all the players, a loose description of the assembled group, was a plus point personally, but would this work on the pitch?

The soccer supremo who had painstakingly recruited me informed me that I was to play on the right side of midfield. Déjà vu! It was shortly after this that I found out that my signing spared him from playing. At this point I should add that this guy was unbelievably lazy in life and lived off his dole money and was probably incapable of running at all. He also had a stunning resemblance to Shaggy from *Scooby-Doo!*

Players turned up sill dressed for the nightclubs the previous night and hoped pals had picked up their kit on the way. Others were still drinking from the night before. Some were asleep in the back of cars. Within the hour we were trotting out on the pitch.

Ninety minutes later we crawled off beaten by six goals. Back to the pub! Sunday lunchtime was now added to the daily visits, followed by home for the *Big Match* and a sleep in the bath.

As time went on I realised several things about Edmonton Green. Star player was a bloke called Nicky who played up front. Apparently as a teenager he had trials with Spurs as a goalkeeper, was bombed out for being too short and refused to play in goal again. He was a decent player, but again a bit short to lead the line in all honesty. As the talented one, his influence was huge on the team. He took the free kicks, corners, throw-ins and probably cut the oranges up for half-time!

Alongside him was Pat, an absolute lunatic. Imagine a

stereotypical thirty-year-old Irishman standing over six feet tall with a short fuse. That was Pat! Many times on the pitch with the ball down our end, upon clearing it we would see the opposing central defender flat out on the floor. Most of the time nobody would see what had taken place, but we all knew. Off the pitch he was the quietest, gentlest man you could wish to meet. Give him a cigar and a Guinness and Pat was content. The funniest thing about him was his cars. He had a passion for those dreadful old Citroens with the split side windows. Pat looked like a bear in a circus car!

In midfield we were blessed with the two Mickeys, Dolly and the Wicks brothers. Mental Mickey was strong as an ox, brave as a lion and had the touch of an elephant. Pretty Mickey always brought his poor girlfriend to watch him play and spent most of the time trying to impress her by rolling around on the floor. Believe me, Ronaldo and Drogba are not in his league! Dolly was one of our better players, but needed fifty chances to score. Dave Wicks was a Vernon Kay look-alike, but played liked Danny Kaye, whilst brother Pete was a willing player, but lacked quality, like most of us.!

In goal we alternated between Webby, Shrimps and Yiddo. Webby was unreliable in his commitment to getting out of bed, Shrimps became disillusioned at picking the ball out of the net and packed up, whilst Yiddo was enthusiastic, but too short to reach the crossbar at full stretch. Some choice!

Despite being voted Man of the Match on my debut, I moved to right back and found I could do a decent job there. Alongside me in defence were Skippy, Blackie and Maths. Together we became the strength of the team and, although we lost most games, the four of us always put a good shift in. Skippy worked in a bank and never wanted to get his face marked as it caused him problems there. Playing central defence didn't help avoiding that. Maths was the coolest player in the team, always having time on the ball and looking to play football rather than lumping it long. For a while he played in midfield, but other teams kicked him off the park so he dropped back into defence. Blackie was unpredictable. Always there, sometimes terrific, sometimes hung-over and always argumentative.

So that was Edmonton Green F.C. A squad lacking in ability, but blessed with solidarity. Over the next seven years or so we became a family, all be it a dysfunctional one! Almost weekly there would be a skirmish on the pitch and everybody got involved. Nobody backed down and we were all there for each other. The bond between us was special and if somehow we could have added some talent we would have been unstoppable!

Personally, I had improved my game immensely, my stamina being a huge asset. From nowhere I developed at bit of pace and my control was tidy. I was growing up so my strength was improving all the time. I learnt to impose myself on my direct opponent and not let him impose himself on me. Usually, this would be a nippy little sod, so the first chance I got in every match I would look to introduce myself. He might get past me, the ball might get past me, but guaranteed they wouldn't both get past! On some occasions I would miss both and on those days I knew I was in for a torrid ninety minutes.

At the pub we were well liked. We spent lots of money, behaved well most of the time and respected the elders such as Bert, an old war veteran, who never needed to put his hand in his pocket if any of the team were in the pub.

Behind the bar was the old bell for ringing time at the end of the night. We adopted it and, after rare victories, would take turns in getting our hands on it to 'ring the victory bell'.

As a club, money was tight and we continually ended up putting in our own money to pay pitch fees and expenses. Damages to the pub's windows also had to be covered on more than one occasion as the Sunday morning warm up started by belting the ball against the pub wall playing a game we called 'fives' which involved kicking the ball across the main road at times.

One of the ways we raised money was the annual sponsored pub crawl. The idea was to partake in refreshments at as many pubs as possible in an evening, get your card signed by the landlord and move on. Infallible!

Every crawl ended in disaster. Fighting with a gang of skinheads was the worst, with the best probably being when only half the team needed to be carried home. The club never made any money through any of the crawls as all the money went on the beer and all we succeeded in doing was getting banned from several pubs. Fortunately, we always chose areas that we didn't really go to much so that wasn't a huge loss.

Back on the pitch we were picking up fines for our committed attitude. Amazingly, my only red card came for swearing at the ref after he wrongly blew up for handball against me. Initially, it was a yellow card, but having been wronged, I wouldn't shut up, threw the ball at him and saw the red card instead. That cost me a £12 fine and thirty day ban, although we got round that as I took the name and place of the injured Blackie for the duration of the ban.

Mental Mickey showed the all for one spirit in one game. Already sent off for his part in an earlier scuffle he was watching from the touchline drinking a can of lager. Another fight broke out on the pitch and, as Mickey was standing closest to the incident, he was the first one there bringing his beer can down on the opponent's head leaving him out cold. All out warfare followed with managers and fans involved. The game was abandoned by the ref who didn't sign up for the WWF and the fighting continued in the changing rooms, luckily not ours as they were ripped apart. A huge fine and a warning about our future conduct followed and a cup draw against the same team inside a couple of weeks, which somehow passed with no repeat of the trouble.

One Sunday, I got what I deserved in a round about way. A couple of weeks previously I had clashed with an opponent and the verbals continued after the game with threats issued for the return match. On the day, however, this guy was playing in his team's back four, miles away from me and the fifty-fifty tackle I wanted looking unlikely. Then we got a corner. My chance! As the ball was sent in I started my run, in his direction, until I realised the ball was coming perfect for me to head at goal. Caught in two minds I failed to see the keeper flying through the air towards me. I soon felt him! I was brought round with smelling salts, covered in blood, with concussion, a broken nose and my teeth through my lip!

Things weren't always thuggish and we strived to improve technically, but we just couldn't step up a level as a team. Goals were always a problem, at both ends. Up top, because we had little firepower, and at the back due to the relentless pressure we were forced to defend. Indeed, in over seven seasons I scored a meagre three goals. Stopping them go in was my main job, but I should have had a better return.

I was fortunate with injury, never missing any games. I had the obvious cuts and bruises and the broken nose previously mentioned, but was not expecting what was around the corner. Three games into a new season and amazingly unbeaten! Trotting up the pitch to support the attack I turned my ankle in a divot in the pitch. As soon as it happened I knew it was bad. The pain told me that much! A trip to the hospital gave me the worst news. "Torn ankle ligaments son! Here's some crutches and don't expect to play again this season!"

"What! This is my life, I can't stop playing!" The crutches were hardly used and I pushed myself to the limit to get back. I can empathise with any player on the comeback trail. The doubts are constantly there whatever you say out loud. For me, playing was my weekly fix built around travelling with the Spurs and work commitments. For a professional it is their career. In any situation it is character building and mentally testing.

Anyway, I made it back to full fitness within about six months, but had no club to play for. Edmonton Green had folded due to inability to fulfil fixtures. Several players had picked up injuries, some had moved away and a few had settled down with partners and Sunday morning football no longer fitted into their lives. It was a pity the club ended the way it did as we were so close. To my knowledge nobody left for another club in the whole time I was there despite our poor position in the tables. That speaks volumes for what we shared.

I played a handful of games for a Turkish team in an all Turkish league for a close friend, Shaban, who told me to keep my mouth shut and I would pass for a Turk as I was dark featured! The football was brutal and any tackle below chin height seemed legal to them. Those few games took me to the end of the season and, from then on, I never joined another team. I have played in works matches and tournaments, charity Christmas matches and still played five-a-side three times a week until I moved away from London a few years ago. The ankle is perfect and only troubles me with slight swelling after I've played or trained the youth team. I can live with that!

I never looked for another team after Edmonton Green. I'm not sure why. It doesn't matter now; it's gone, but I wouldn't have missed a second of what we shared together. Every kick, every goal conceded, every morning putting nets up still hungover and every laugh. It was a wonderful time and I grew up through it. I went from a sixteen-year-old boy to a young confident man. I learnt to look after myself and my own. I gave, and received, respect.

In short, I loved it all and wouldn't have changed any of it!

CHAPTER 10 – MANAGERS
The hottest seat

Who would be a football manager?

It's a much asked question that only those that have done the job can answer. From World Cup winners to the guy who picks the school team, they all have one thing in common. They all have the desire to be involved in the game after they have hung up their boots.

For me, it was about improving the youngsters and gradually seeing the ugly duckling turn into a swan. I also wanted to improve the club on the previous season's performance. This is something I achieved every season and something I am very proud of.

The challenge to pick a winning team, and successfully change it if it wasn't working, is also a factor for most.

Modern day football has changed the way a manager is allowed to run a football club. Once upon a time, a manger would be given years at a club to try to bring success to it. He would have complete control and be in charge of not only team selection and training, but transfers, wages and, probably, if the kit lady used Daz or Persil! In this era, managerial giants stood out like Matt Busby, Bill Nicholson and Bill Shankly. Respectively, at Manchester United, Tottenham and Liverpool, they were given the time to put in place everything required to bring unprecedented success to those clubs. Their impact on the clubs, and indeed football, is there for all to see in the record books.

It wasn't just the trophies they piled up that makes them stand out from the rest. All three can be classed as pioneers. Busby was the first manager to take an English team into the European Cup, and ten years after the Munich air crash, the first to win it.

Nicholson was the first to achieve the league and cup double, and also the first to win a European trophy. Shankly took the then smaller of the Merseyside teams, at the time, by the scruff of the neck and set the ball rolling for twenty years of glory.

The only problem for these clubs, was who on earth could follow them when they stepped down? United and Spurs both got it badly wrong and appointed the wrong successors. Both were relegated within a couple of years of losing Busby and Nicholson.

It is strange how different clubs act at times and looking at these three clubs shows exactly that. Busby stepped upstairs, but his presence was too big for the men that followed, O'Farrell couldn't cope, Docherty, Sexton and Atkinson were largely unsuccessful, and over a decade passed until Fergie rolled up to begin his own dynasty.

At Tottenham, the board treated Bill Nick disgracefully and completely cast this legend aside when he stepped down. Bill was reduced to scouting for West Ham instead of still playing a part at his beloved White Hart Lane. He even had his home a couple of hundred yards from the ground. Thankfully, when a new board came to the club they got him back at the club, working behind the scenes.

Nicholson's advice regarding a replacement was ignored and Terry Neill was brought in instead; a man who played for, and loved, Arsenal. Neill, in my opinion, is responsible for our relegation, even though he had left the club a year before we went down. Oh, by the way, he went back to Arsenal!

Liverpool, on the other hand, got it so, so right when Shankly called it a day. Part of Shankly's legacy was the famous Anfield boot room. Along with his coaching team, he would sit and discuss football over a cup of tea for hours on end. When Shanks left, the club promoted Bob Paisley from the boot room. Paisley took the club to new heights with European Cup glory and total dominance in the league. When he left, Joe Fagan stepped up from the boot room and did exactly the same. Promotion from within the club followed with Kenny Dalglish becoming player-manager, and Roy Evans from the boot room also. Continuity was the key to Liverpool's success. The last twenty years has not seen a league title at Anfield but it has seen the end of the boot room. Coincidence? I don't think so!

In recent years there have been very few examples of a club promoting from within, with most clubs desperate for immediate success, and not willing to take a chance on an untried manager. Admittedly, some number twos are not able to step up to the main job, and some do not want to.

Sunderland's Ricky Sbragia has openly admitted how much he hated his year in charge and couldn't wait to get back into the background. Brian Kidd spent years under Fergie at United, took the manager's job at Blackburn and didn't have a clue what he was doing.

Modern managers have a completely different job to the likes of Busby, Shanks and Billy Nick. Instant success is not only desired, but expected with every appointment. Gone are the three-year plans that managers used to try to work to. Success needs to happen...now!

Some clubs and owners seem to have expectations that are way above their level. Manchester City are an easy target at the moment with their owners expecting the title to be delivered. All the money they are throwing at the team will not guarantee the title. They need a solid team, not a collection of big money signings and I hope the title doesn't find its way back to them anytime soon. Mark Hughes had the club moving in the right direction, but lost his job after two defeats. Madness! City had not won the league in over forty years and nothing at all for over thirty. Why did they think glory is an entitlement?

Over the last few seasons City have won the title twice, the FA Cup and the League Cup, or whatever it is called these days. Money made it happen without a doubt, but Mancini and Pellegrini were both cast aside despite winning titles. Pep Guardiola is about to pick up the reigns at the club. His record is outstanding, but has he proved himself yet? I do not believe he has. This is his first test in my opinion. Titles with Barcelona in a two-team league and Bayern in a one-team league were almost guaranteed. If he does it in England, with several other contenders, I will accept that he is special.

Constant changing of a manager will seldom bring any success. Short term it may see an improvement in results, but if the manager is then replaced the next season, how can any team settle into a pattern of playing?

West Ham are a club that had a seriously low number of managers in their history with Ron Greenwood and John Lyall holding the reigns for years. In recent years, I have completely lost track of just how many have been in charge for a year or two!

West Ham have always played football the right way and have a good history, even if they have not seen much silverware. That is their level! Constant changes of their manager is not going to change that. Sadly, they are also now seen as a selling club and all of their home grown talent disappears out of the door as soon as a big club waves a cheque at them! Maybe that will change under Bilic and the move to the Olympic Stadium.

At the other end of the scale are Chelsea. Chelsea are similar in background and history to West Ham, but with more silverware from past glories. I know Chelsea supporters who cannot name all of their managers in the last ten years. And they are in the best run of success that they have ever had. The way they get through managers is similar to how the likes of Real Madrid operate. Win or out, and out even if you win! Chelsea are now established as one of the top clubs in the country and in the hunt for every trophy they compete for. Their consistency is due to the strength of the team as much as anything any manager has done in the last decade.

Directors of football have been tried and, in the main, failed as the person appointed really wants the manager's job. There can be only one boss! Most managers these days are given the brief to deal with the squad and that's it. Transfer targets are passed to the chairman and he does the negotiating. Wages are not the concern of the manager. In some cases, the manager will leave the coaching to somebody else and never be seen on the training ground.

With such an influx of foreign managers, the game in this country was always going to change. Many sides play not to win, but to avoid defeat at all costs. This must be bred into them from the game in their own country and I suppose it is understandable to a degree. If you are an Italian with years of negative football designed to achieve a 1-0 win, then our gung ho football must be difficult to adapt to.

But, if you bite the bullet and come to England to manage, one thing you have to do is learn the language! Managers like Arsene Wenger, Rafa Benitez and Sven understood this obvious challenge and learnt the language quickly and well. Others like Fabio Capello, after over two years here, still seem to be stuck on the basics and most of what they say makes little sense. Hmm, maybe that explains the World Cup in Africa!

So, what makes a good manager or indeed, a great manager? Why can some ex-players make the grade easily and some fail miserably? Bobby Charlton and Bobby Moore both failed to cut it as managers after glorious playing careers, while Alex Ferguson and Arsene Wenger hardly pulled up any trees as players, but are the two most successful managers in the last twenty years. Jose Mourinho has won titles in Portugal, England, Spain and Italy and a few Champions Leagues as well, but who remembers his playing days apart from him? I recently found an old press photo of Louis Van Gaal being turned inside out by Johann Cruyff. I didn't even know Van Gaal had played!

In days long since passed, a manager would learn his trade in the lower leagues and progress to the bigger jobs slowly. Many players now finish their careers as a player and drop straight into a Premiership managerial job. Sometimes it works, other times it is a disaster.

Martin O'Neill gained valuable experience at non-league level and Wycombe before success at Leicester. Celtic followed and then Villa before the Republic of Ireland. Slow progression from a very good manager brought up under Brian Clough.

On the other side of the coin, John Barnes had a glorious career but, since hanging up his boots, he has failed at Celtic, Tranmere and God knows what he was doing with Jamaica! Gone are the days when a manager had a trusty sidekick and took on the world like Brian Clough and Peter Taylor. Now a manager has more assistants than players it seems!

Not digging at Harry Redknapp at all here because, in two years, he took Tottenham from propping up the league to the Champions League, but why did he need so many people on the bench with him? Bond, Jordan, Allen, Parks, Sherwood, Ferdinand, and that's without the kit man, doctor and the rest!

The role of the manager has certainly changed over the years and only one can win the league in any given season. They are always the person to blame when it goes wrong, or even when it goes right in some cases, so I repeat my opening line…who would be a football manager?

CHAPTER 11 – ENGLAND
A little glory and a load of pain

Once upon a time, playing for your country was the pinnacle of a player's career. I'm not sure that applies in the modern game. As the Premiership and Champions League dominate our game, playing for England seems to matter less and less and performances seem to back that up. Why?

As a fan, I struggle to raise any interest in an England friendly when twenty years ago I would have been there after looking forward to it for weeks. I am fiercely patriotic and want England to win at everything, even sports like cricket which I have no interest in. If England are playing, I want them to win. Pulling on the three lions should still mean everything to a player, but as I said earlier, doesn't seem to anymore. Where is the passion and pride?

There are obvious exceptions like David Beckham. You could see how passionate he was about his country, but he appears to be in the minority. I cannot understand how any player can retire from international football while they are still playing for their clubs. If selected, play! Why turn your back on your country?

I can understand it when a player is at the end of his career and starts to pick up injuries and takes longer to recover. There is a need, in those circumstances, to protect yourself and prolong your playing days. That excuse is not there for others who have quit their country.

Paul Scholes should have had an extra five years for England, but walked away. Jamie Carragher walked away TWICE! Why was he ever invited back for a World Cup jolly? With the goalkeepers' shirt a problem, Paul Robinson turned his back on a call up. The fact that he was treated poorly for two years before should not have led to his international retirement.

Years ago, David Bentley claimed he was too tired to play for his country. Raheem Sterling has since said the same. They want to do a week or two on a building site, or a market, or down the pits. Then they can be tired! Chris Sutton refused to play for England B around the same time claiming he was too good for them and should be in the full squad. In my opinion, he was one of the luckiest players to ever be included in an England squad and England B was an over achievement. These, and the other players I have forgotten who quit their country, are a disgrace.

England has also been hurt by the devaluation of an international cap. We can thank Sven for that! Mass substitutions during friendly matches under him meant many players will show in the record books as England players that would never have been there under normal circumstances. The games turned into a farce with continual changes too and I believe that this is where I lost my interest in England friendlies.

Elsewhere, I have covered World Cups, but England have had terrible luck at some and completely lost the plot at others. We always seem to take unfit players too! Keegan, Brooking, Beckham, Rooney, Robson, Barry, Henderson,…why? As good a player as these guys were, if they were not fit, they should have stayed at home.

The FA has a hell of a lot to answer for over the years, with the choices they have made regarding the managers they have appointed. Also suspect, are some of the crazy contracts they have awarded these guys making it impossible to sack them because of the payoff implications. Why extend a contract before a major tournament? Capello was the luckiest manager in world football after Africa. Totally inept, but sitting on such a huge contract the FA couldn't afford to pay him off.

Since Sir Alf Ramsey, the faceless wonders have selected eleven men to manage the national team. I believe half of them were the wrong choice and only three can be called a success. Picking the right man is crucial and, for years, the right man was Brian

Clough. Unfortunately, the FA bottled it every time he was in the frame. Meanwhile, Clough took two nothing teams, Derby and Forest, to league titles and Forest to back to back European titles and a few other cups. In the same time span, England won bugger all and failed to even qualify for two World Cups!

Qualification for World Cups and European Championships should be a bare minimum requirement for us surely, not something to celebrate. We are England not Liechtenstein!

So, back to the men who have been given the poison chalice since Sir Alf was hounded out after that terrible night when 'a clown' kept us out of the World Cup in 1974. The appointment of Don Revie was as good as England could have made at the time. His Leeds team had been at the top of our game for a decade and similar was expected at international level.

Revie had instilled a family ethic at Leeds upon which much of their success was founded. Unfortunately, with England, he treated many players like the relatives you don't want to visit. Players like Currie, Ball, Hudson, MacDonald and George were all deemed unnecessary to requirements. Failure to qualify for the Euros in 1976 was followed by an uphill task to reach the World Cup in 1978. Revie turned his back on the challenge and, on the back of a five match winless run in 1977, took a fortune to manage in Dubai.

Revie left us in the lurch and was forever remembered a traitor, all his club achievements forgotten. The FA should have gone for Cloughie at this point, but instead went for Mr Nice! Ron Greenwood was a choice that would not offend anybody after the mess Revie had caused. Clough was too much of a loose cannon and may have caused embarrassment. Who cares? He might have won something! Greenwood was a fabulous manager at West Ham, but had limited success and nice guys don't often win do they?

In fairness to him, Greenwood took us to the Euros in 1980, but failed to get out of the group and also made it to the World Cup in 1982 where we returned home unbeaten. Two draws in the second group stage saw us eliminated.

My lasting memory of Greenwood would be that he was indecisive. He alternated Peter Shilton and Ray Clemence in goal until his last five games in charge. He gave a debut to Glenn Hoddle, but then didn't have the courage to stick with him. At least he brought decency back to the England set up.

The other good thing that he did was to bring some club managers into the England fold, by giving them Under-21 or B-team duties. This was an excellent idea and the two managers who have made it to World Cup and European Championship Semi-Finals with England, were involved in this. Knowing the England set up must have been an advantage before they stepped into the top job surely? Why did we stop doing it?

Next up was Bobby Robson. Bobby would survive vicious media assaults to become a national treasure during his eight-year reign. Robson was not the nation's choice, that was still Clough, but he was a winner. His Ipswich side had been title contenders for a few seasons and lifted cups at home and in Europe.

He started by ending England legend Kevin Keegan's England career. That made him unpopular right from the start, but he turned things around with two strong World Cups in 1986 and 1990 when we could have won it. In between, he survived a press hate campaign, off field revelations about his personal life and a poor European championship. Bobby won titles, after England, in Spain, Portugal and Holland proving to all his pedigree was of the highest quality. For England he was the nearly man.

This was surely the last chance for Brian Clough, but no. Graham Taylor was the next man in and, once again, I have to question the choice. Taylor had been successful in lower league football before taking Watford to the top flight where they more than held their own. A decent spell at Aston Villa followed before the FA came calling.

His term will be remembered by many for three things. The turnip headline with his face on it, printed by *The Sun* at the height of the hate campaign against him, and the disastrous tournament at Euro 1992 where England were awful. His poor relationship with captain Gary Lineker, was at its most obvious in the final game, when he withdrew him when we needed a goal so desperately.

But above all else, Taylor will be remembered for his 'Do I not like that' documentary. Somehow the FA and Taylor agreed that a TV crew could follow him around during the unsuccessful World Cup qualification process. I watched the DVD again recently and it really is like watching somebody having a breakdown! Taylor was a good club manager, but England boss. Never!

The people's choice had now shifted away from Brian Clough and the man the nation wanted was Terry Venables. We got him! El Tel had the football world at his feet. His managerial track record could boast strong spells at QPR and Crystal Palace before winning the Spanish title with Barcelona. His spell at Tottenham was mixed, but he still had an FA Cup win to show for it, despite crippling debts which turned us into a selling club.

Venables had the good fortune of automatic qualification for Euro 96 due to England being the host nation. What a tournament we had, beating the Scots and showing Holland what total football meant in the nineties, before losing on penalties to the Germans in the semi-final.

Surely Venables was here to stay, but no! Off field business which led to court hearings meant he had to step down to clear his name. The FA should have done more to keep him, even if it would have meant getting a caretaker in until he could resume. Once again, they made the wrong choice and let him go.

Next to wear the crown was Glenn Hoddle. Hoddle was quite a popular choice and, in my opinion, is the man who put the foundations in place for the rise of Chelsea. On the negative side, Hoddle the manager was seen as aloof and on the training ground saw himself as a better player still than those he was picking to play! A decent World Cup in France, after a magnificent result in Italy to get there in the first place, saw the challenge end with Beckham's red card against Argentina. As valiantly as the ten men battled, we failed on penalties, again!

The future looked bright, but somehow Hoddle imploded. Already derided by press and players for his insistence that the players had sessions with his faith healer, Hoddle was criticised for releasing a World Cup diary, revealing secrets from within the camp.

Personally, I think that there was a witch-hunt from within the FA for Hoddle at this point. I own World Cup diaries by both Ron Greenwood and two by Bobby Robson as well as several by players. I do not remember any problem raised by the FA regarding those!

Anyway, Hoddle needed to keep his head down for a bit, instead he incredibly committed football suicide. At a press conference he gave an insight to his religious beliefs and stated that handicapped people must have done something in a previous life to deserve their fate in this life! The FA had their excuse, Hoddle was gone! Two excellent managers on the trot gone for non-footballing reasons! Do we want to win things or not?

Another popular choice followed, but within two years Kevin Keegan had gone, admitting he was out of his depth. In many ways I respected his total honesty that wet, miserable day we had been beaten by Germany but, in other ways, I felt the timing was awful. We still had other qualifiers to play including one within a few days.

The Keegan reign was built on passion and very little else in all honesty, so the next man in needed to incorporate some tactical knowledge into the mix. At this point the FA finally became bold and made a controversial appointment. Sven Goran Eriksson became the first non-English England manager. Now maybe I'm a bit old school here, but in my book the England manager should be English! I can understand small Arabic or African countries looking for foreign managers, but not the big names in world football. Especially not us.

Sven came with a lot of promise and did a decent job until we reached the finals of competitions. Once again, we were found wanting tactically when it really mattered. He was totally incapable of changing from his set playing pattern and somehow managed to grasp defeat from the hands of victory at two World Cups! He put too much faith in the same players and would pick them all the time. Considering his overuse of substitutes, it is incredible he didn't find more new talent.

As time went on it became obvious that the FA had really screwed it up this time. Sven got caught up in scandals with women, got caught on tape discussing taking a job with a fake sheikh, but was tied to such a good contract we couldn't afford to get rid of him! When the time came for a replacement, the FA screwed it up again.

At least Steve McClaren was English, but very much a part of Sven's regime. Indeed, he kept faith with most of Sven's team and failed to qualify for the Euros! I truly believe that he is the worst choice the FA has ever made to lead our country and the results back me up. The lasting image of this guy is the sight of him standing under an umbrella as we got beaten by Croatia at Wembley in a match that ended our hopes of qualification. It is no coincidence that he had to go abroad to try to rebuild his career.

Next another foreigner, this time Italian Fabio Capello. Following a strong qualification for the World Cup, things looked like we had a winner here. What evolved in Africa was a shambles beyond our wildest imaginations and I have documented this elsewhere.

Sadly, it appeared he learned nothing from the experience. Still no communication, proved by including players in his first squad after the World Cup who then informed him, thanks but no thanks. Michael Carrick was left out of the squad because Capello thought he was injured. He wasn't! Does this man not possess a telephone? Several players were excluded from that squad who were non-playing members of that World Cup squad or in the back up squad. Weeks before Capello had thought they were in the top thirty players in England, but were discarded without playing.

His apparent ending of David Beckham's England career when he blurted it out in an interview was shocking. Beckham has given his all for England, was part of the Olympic bid and also at the forefront of our World Cup bid for 2018. To be treated like that stinks! Capello faced an uphill battle from here to turn the tide. The fans and the press had lost faith and he was a dead man walking!

Roy Hodgson was next.

Nice guy, decent manager, but was he really going to succeed where the rest failed? He survived a dreadful World Cup in Brazil, but could not survive the defeat by Iceland in the Euros. "I don't know what I am doing here," is a comment that will live with him for the rest of his life. Sorry Roy, but we didn't either!

As I write, Sam Allardyce has just left the post after one game and less than two months in the job.

After getting caught up in a newspaper "sting", there was no alternative.

I think it's a shame for England, because although he was not my choice, I liked a lot of the things he was bringing to the table. Sam was always at the front when new innovations came into the game throughout his career and it might have been good to have somebody with a no nonsense approach in charge. Sadly, we will never know.

So who is next? Above all else, I hope it is an Englishman.

I wouldn't be averse to a manager from other parts of Britain like Martin O'Neill or Mark Hughes although that's probably a nonstarter. These sort of people understand our league, our players and our temperament. We are different to Europeans.

Gareth Southgate has been given the job on a temporary basis covering four matches, but what happens then?

Anything less than four wins out of four will probably end his reign.

Glenn Hoddle returning is being spoken about, possibly with

Harry Redknapp by his side. Most fans would be happy with that, but personally I don't believe the FA will go for them as they carry baggage. Heaven forbid that they know the game inside out!

Eddie Howe is too young, but definitely one for the future, Steve Bruce and Alan Pardew have all been mentioned.

What about this for a real long shot? Stick with Southgate, but bring in Hoddle as a wise head to guide him.

Add David Beckham and Stuart Pearce to the backroom team also.

Beckham is a terrific ambassador for the game and Pearce has managerial experience. Both are fiercely patriotic and have had long distinguished careers. Can you imagine players being called up by these two? Their pride is obvious to all and they can fill a room with their caps and medals.

At the same time, look to the future and give Eddie Howe a role with the Under 21's so he gets a feel for International football whilst still learning at Bournemouth.

It might just work you know!

CHAPTER 12 – FOREIGNERS
The beautiful invasion

When I started to follow football in the late sixties the only foreigners in our game were Scots, Irish and Welsh. Anybody from overseas was only seen in European competition or on limited TV newsreels.

In the same way that people remember where they were when they heard Princess Diana was dead or JFK had been assassinated, I remember where I was when Tottenham introduced foreigners to English football. I was on a coach, on a day trip to France, and had picked up a newspaper to pass the time on the journey. The headline screamed out at me. SPURS SIGN WORLD CUP WINNERS!

My first thought was Mario Kempes, the goalscoring sensation whose goals had done so much for Argentina a few weeks previously. As I read on it became apparent that Spurs had signed Osvaldo Ardiles and Riccardo Villa, both midfield players who I remembered well from the World Cup. At first I felt Villa would be more suited to our game, mainly down to his size. Little did I know that both would become legends at the Lane in a few short years. Neither did I realise that our signings would open the floodgates to the point that league matches would take place with no Englishmen playing within a couple of decades!

There was a media frenzy over the next few weeks as everybody and his dog had an opinion on foreign imports. 'Shouldn't be allowed', screamed some while others praised manager Keith Burkinshaw for his bold move. Some claimed they wouldn't last until Christmas.

I can remember the excitement as we headed up the M6 for the first game of the season. Spurs were back in the top flight after a twelve month stint in Division Two, the opponents that day? Nottingham Forest, Champions of England. Talk about in at the deep end!

The mixture of excitement and nerves were not helped that day as our coach drove into the back of a car and we thought we would miss the match. Fortunately, we arrived at the ground and Tottenham were everywhere. God knows how many fans made the trip that day but we outnumbered Forest big time. As the team trotted out we gave them the ticker tape welcome that Argentinian fans had done throughout the World Cup. It was awesome that this was in England and for OUR team!

Ricky got off to a perfect start, as did Tottenham, with our goal in a deserved 1-1 draw, but his greatest day was still three years away. The 1981 FA Cup Final, two goals in the replay, detailed in depth elsewhere in this book. Ossie started slower, but showed his amazing talent much more consistently over the years, forming a great partnership with Glenn Hoddle for many seasons.

In the following few seasons more clubs followed Tottenham's lead. It had worked for us so others began to look abroad for new blood. Ipswich, then a top side, went Dutch with Muhren and Thijssen and almost won the title. Several clubs picked up bargains from Scandinavia and soon there were many countries represented in our league.

Not all were successful, and to this day that is true. Lots of substandard players came into our game and, quite simply, were a waste of money. For every Ronaldo or Zola there have been several Marco Boogers turning up in our league.

The problems began when clubs started to fill their teams with foreign talent. UEFA made a stand and limited clubs to three on the pitch in European competitions but, as usual, messed it up by rating Scots, Irish and Welsh as foreign. This was obviously a severe handicap to English teams and, along with the ban for Heysel, the reason why our domination of Europe waned for over a decade.

Another problem with lots of imports was the impact on the national team. English players were simply not getting enough football. It is still the case. We are in European Championships year at present and in our top flight only four English goalkeepers are first choices. Four out of twenty! Between the sticks used to be our strongest position. I can remember Shilton, Clemence, Corrigan, Parkes all chasing the number one shirt for England at the same time. Paul Cooper from Ipswich and others I have forgotten never got a sniff as the pecking order was so strong in front of them.

Currently our top four are Hart (solid, but under threat of Pep's arrival), Butland (injured), Forster (injury prone) and Heaton (untested at international level and at a yo yo club). Too many imports have caused this, nothing else. The talent is still there, but the chance to show it is less.

England, over the last couple of seasons, have intimated that a foreign player who has been in this country for a number of years would become eligible to play for England. If that day ever comes, I will turn my back on the national team.

Something that the foreign element has brought to our shores, along with glittering skills, is a play acting mentality. I find it really sickening to see the likes of Diego Costa rolling around on the floor in apparent agony when somebody has made the slightest contact with him. Costa is a huge talent and, on his day, one of the best strikers in world football. He is also a giant of a man and why he spends half of every match on the floor is beyond me. I get bumped into when shopping at Asda, but at the point of writing, have still managed to avoid crashing into a pile of vegetables and rolling to the checkouts!

It is the job of the officials and powers that be to eradicate our game of this disease. I have seen at first hand, in youth football, kids rolling around when nobody has touched them. They are copying what they see Costa and company doing. It has to stop!

A lot of imported players are simply mercenaries! They come for the money and are happy to sit on the bench and do nothing for their fifty pieces of silver. Some come for one last pay day before they are put out to graze. Whatever their reasons, I do not blame the players. Who wouldn't do the same if in their position?

I hope I have not come across as negative to foreign imports as I have admired so many of them over the years. Our game is better because of the talent that has crossed the water to play here, I just feel a bit more restriction is needed for the reasons I have stated. When a league game is played in England with no Englishmen involved, something is wrong, that's all!

The Carlos Tevez fiasco is another example of potential problems that should be addressed. Who owns him is so unclear it is a joke. The agent owns the registration so any transfer fee goes through him? West Ham brought him in, played him illegally and he scored the goals to keep them up. Sheffield United went down instead of the Hammers, but even after being told it was illegal stayed relegated? What? Then Tevez goes to Manchester United, wants to stay there, and the club want to keep him, but he moves to Manchester City. You couldn't make it up!

I have nothing but respect for a foreign player who comes to our country, adapts well and stays for many seasons with one club. Jussi Jaskelainen, the ex-Bolton keeper is a good example. He was at the club for several seasons and had many opportunities to move to bigger clubs. It is to his credit that he showed such loyalty to a middle table club as they were at the time.

All the top clubs have benefited from world class imports since Ossie and Ricky pioneered the way. Spurs had Klinnsman and Ginola, Arsenal had Bergkamp, Henry and Viera and Chelsea had Zola, Gullit and Vialli. Liverpool had Torres and United have seen Ronaldo, Cantona and Schmeichel. Even teams like Middlesbrough have had Ravenelli and Juninho.

These and many, many more have been wonderful for our game.

CHAPTER 13 – VIOLENCE
The dark side

When I started going to football matches I was not aware of any trouble. Sure, there was a lot of banter between rival fans, but that was about it. Within a decade violence had taken over the game.

Football became a despised word for many people and the majority of fans were sickened by the actions of some. English clubs were thrown out of Europe and Maggie Thatcher tried to bring in ID cards for all supporters. Ken Bates, then Chelsea chairman, wanted to put electric fences up at Stamford Bridge. Luton Town banned away fans from Kenilworth Road.

Somehow things seemed to settle down after a game where violence was not prominent, but brought tragedy.

The sheer volume of trouble had led to the erection of fences at all top flight grounds, and it is a direct result of these fences that ninety-six Liverpool fans are no longer with us. If those fences had not been in place at Hillsborough in 1989 then the fans would not have been crushed up against them. Somehow football came through these testing times and violence at matches is an exception now and not the norm.

The first time I can recall widespread violence was in 1974 when Tottenham fans rampaged in Holland against Feyenoord. The TV screens showed supporters clashing and police giving out fearsome beatings to anybody in sight.

A year later, I was a lot closer to the trouble when Tottenham and Chelsea fans rioted at White Hart Lane before a vital league match. Hundreds of fans fought each other on the pitch and I do not mind admitting to being quite scared as I too ran onto the pitch. As a fourteen-year-old, my reason for being on the pitch was to get away from the fighting behind me. I had no intention of getting involved!

However, when you go to as many matches as I have attended throughout the most violent times football has faced, you cannot avoid trouble all the time. I never looked for it, but just occasionally it found me! I was attacked by a gang of Liverpool supporters at Anfield and by Manchester United fans at Old Trafford. Both times the attacks came from behind and the first I knew of imminent danger was when a fist caught me! Brave eh? At least when Stoke fans went for me at the old Victoria Ground they came at me from the front. Several of them came at a group of Tottenham fans and all hell broke loose before the police piled in.

The only time I have been badly hurt was, weirdly, nowhere near a football ground! In the late seventies and eighties, it was just as dangerous travelling up the motorway! If Spurs were playing in the Midlands, for example, we would always check to see where the likes of Chelsea or West Ham were travelling to. Most team's fans we bumped into at service stations were no threat as Tottenham took huge numbers to away matches and only a madman would try to take Spurs supporters on when vastly outnumbered. Chelsea and West Ham were supported on a similar scale to Tottenham though and if we stopped at the same place trouble was inevitable.

One night, I was on my way back from Nottingham Forest when we stopped at Newport Pagnell services. Only a few of us had returned to the coach when two coaches full of Chelsea fans pulled in. This was never going to go well! The Chelsea fans smashed all the windows on our coach and then got on the coach lashing out with fence posts at everybody. When you are sat in a seat you cannot fight back and I took several blows and ended up quite bloodied. Our driver was less fortunate and received a broken arm for his troubles! Luckily for us, some Spurs coaches pulled in and quickly set about the Chelsea fans. Not the best night I've ever had! We lost the match 4-0 too.

As I said before, there have been several close shaves over the years. A Nottingham Forest fan that I had been drinking with before a game at the City Ground led me away from another Forest fan who had started an argument with me as we walked to the ground. Apparently, the second fan had a knife in his hand and I was his intended target!

At Leeds, I avoided dozens of batteries and darts being thrown at our group as we walked back to our coach and at Upton Park I swear I have never seen so many bottles flying through the air. I have lost count of the number of times the windows of our coaches were smashed as we left away grounds.

Being a Tottenham fan was an advantage when it came to trouble. Spurs have always had a real hard core of violent fans and reputations get around. Most teams were scared of a Tottenham visit and quite rightly so! A number of Spurs fans would gain entry to the home supporters' end at whatever ground we visited. Just as the match kicked off they would wade into the home fans ridiculously outnumbered. Within seconds they would run hundreds of the home fans out of their own end and take a huge area for themselves until the police escorted them back to the away end.

One day, at Wolves, I made one of the most stupid mistakes of my life. We had been drinking in a pub full of Spurs fans before a game. After reaching the ground a huge number of Wolves fans attacked us and, in the confusion, I found myself outside a pub. Thinking it was the pub I had left minutes before I went back inside only to find it was a Wolves pub. No major problem there you might think, apart from the fact that I was wearing a shirt proclaiming 'Who's afraid of the big bad wolf' on the chest! I do not know how I got away with that one to this day.

As the seasons have passed violence at football matches seems to be a problem away from our shores more than at home. Most European countries have inherited the 'English disease' and are much worse than we are. It is a little bit off that the authorities do not seem to crack down anywhere near as hard as they did on English football thirty years ago! Two Leeds fans were stabbed to death in Turkey. No ban for Turkish clubs followed did it?

Liverpool fans did us no favours rioting at the Heysel Stadium and England fans, to this day, following the national side always seem to get involved in trouble, but it is in no way a one way street. When I used to go to England matches at Wembley I witnessed club rivalries spilling over. Before one international, Tottenham and Middlesbrough fans clashed in one of the bars leaving it totally wrecked. It was so common in those days that I never saw any reports anywhere of what was a bloody clash.

Some of the most infamous games I can recall involved Millwall. For such a small team they really have a hard core following! Most people remember the riot at Luton when Millwall took on the Bedfordshire police force on the pitch, but fewer seem to recall when they went on a rampage during a cup tie against Ipswich. I recall that being just as bad.

During our season in Division Two, in the late seventies, a TV documentary following Millwall was screened. The so called leader of the Millwall hard core was interviewed. 'Harry the Dog' claimed Tottenham were in for a right pasting when the clubs met that Boxing Day. Spurs took masses to the match marching in from London Bridge and, apart from a skirmish here and there, nothing really happened. At the return fixture I have never seen so much trouble outside White Hart Lane, as police struggled to contain the fighting. I will admit that Millwall ran Tottenham close that day!

Not many teams came to Tottenham and gave us any real problems, apart from the London sides I have already mentioned, so I was surprised when Glasgow Rangers came to the Lane for a pre-season friendly and treated it like war, in the eighties. Obviously, I knew that the Scots could be a bit lively, but this lot were on a mission that day for a game that meant nothing.

During my time travelling with the Spurs, I have seen a lot of violence. Nowadays a football match is a much safer place to go to than when I was there week in, week out. Much of the trouble is pre-planned between rival supporters miles away from the ground. Hopefully, it will stay away from the grounds in future.

As a teenager I used to wear Doc Marten boots and it always amused me that the police would make me take my laces out before entering the ground. As soon as we were on the terrace, we would all put them back in. Pointless!

Police in that era would spoil for trouble, especially at away games, and I have seen many instances of this. They would deliberately goad Tottenham fans to provoke a response and then wade in to give a slap or two. Police dogs would 'accidentally' be allowed to get close enough to bite a supporter by the dog handler. A policeman friend of mine once told me that the police were as up for a fight as the fans and couldn't wait for the potential trouble matches to come around.

So, in my opinion, who were the hardest? I have to say that Spurs are right up there and I never saw any team take us out in a big way. Having said that, Chelsea and West Ham were also up there and always caused trouble at the Lane. Both were hard core. Millwall were hard, but not as big as the previous two, so our meetings were few and far between. Arsenal had little to offer and it was an annual event that Tottenham would take the North Bank with little resistance. Certain away grounds would always concern me, such as Leeds and Manchester City, and the further north you went the more you were hated! With England, I can only recall the Welsh and Irish having a right go at Wembley. The Scots completely took over, but were not there for a fight.

In recent years, some of the hard men from different firms have gone into print to reveal their exploits. Trevor Tanner, Cass Pennant and the Brimson brothers to name just a few. I must admit that I have found their books accurate about the time that I was travelling. What I have found lacking in realism is football violence films on the big screen. Let's face it, *The Football factory* and *Green Street* are crap! The best effort I have seen is a little known film called *I.D.* which followed an undercover cop infiltrating a firm and ultimately getting hooked on football violence. Even this film was way off the mark of what it was really like though.

Although football violence is not completely a thing from another era, it is definitely in remission. Football is better for that, and safer!

CHAPTER 14 – WEMBLEY
The home of football

Wembley Stadium. Home of English football. The Holy Grail for all players and supporters alike. They called it the venue of legends and how accurate that title has been over the years. Many players never get there, many clubs don't either, but everybody wants to taste the atmosphere and become part of the tradition. I consider myself very fortunate to have attended Cup Finals and countless international matches at Wembley over the years, tasting unforgettable glory and indescribable pain, sometimes in the same matches!

My first experience of Wembley came in 1972 when my local non-league team, Enfield, faced Hendon in the then named Amateur Cup Final. I cannot recall how it came to be that I was at that final, only that my nan had somehow got tickets for us both. The coach trip was unmemorable until the Twin Towers came into sight. I do remember being underwhelmed with the ground itself that day. Maybe it was because it was only half full, but I was not impressed with the tired paintwork and tatty-looking wooden benches that seemed to run forever.

Enfield failed to deliver that day also and lost 2-0 and the only thing I can remember about the match itself was a Hendon player having the ball blasted into his midriff and needing treatment directly in front of my seat. Strange the things that stick in your mind.

It was to be nine years before my next Cup Final at Wembley and how different this visit was to be. By now I had been to Wembley many times for England matches and my first impressions of the stadium had been changed forever. A capacity Wembley was an awesome place to be, with those huge steps behind the goals giving a terrific view from wherever you stood. The walk up Wembley Way, drawing you in to the ground. Intoxicating you with the nerve-tingling atmosphere. The noise, the expectancy, the dreams!

Throughout the seventies I had hardly missed a Spurs home game and, for about five years, I had been travelling around the country, week in, week out, wherever we were playing, but this was the big one; the FA Cup Final! Tottenham Hotspur back at Wembley and I was there.

Traditionally, Spurs always won something when the year ended in one so all season the Spurs faithful had been expectant, 1981 was also the Chinese year of the cockerel. Everything added up. Our name was on the cup!

Even the path to Wembley had been smoother than we could have hoped. Second Division Queens Park Rangers, Third Division Hull and lowly Coventry were dispatched before Third Division Exeter went the same way in the quarter-finals. The semi-final at Hillsborough against Wolves was the only trip outside London and even the replay was down the road at Highbury. How sweet that victory had been! Waiting at Wembley was Manchester City. City had finished just below us in the league and both sides had won their home match against the other that season.

We left White Hart Lane early on our coaches, all decorated accordingly, in high spirits. Nothing would stop us today! In truth, it was such a short trip the coach was unnecessary, but my mates and I had travelled everywhere together that season and this was the icing on the cake and we wanted to share it together. Soon we were there and a few beers later we were in the stadium singing our hearts out with only thoughts of victory. I was holding aloft my homemade flag, which I still have to this day, THFC PRIDE OF LONDON with Union Jacks in each corner and cockerels in between. I know I will never throw it out; it is part of me and my memories.

Then things began to backfire! The game started and Spurs were not playing the fluent football that had got them there in the first place. Ossie Ardiles, Glenn Hoddle and Ricky Villa couldn't get time on the ball. Up front Steve Archibald and Garth Crooks had no supply and it was the defence that were the busiest players on the pitch. City grew in confidence and took the lead through Tommy Hutchinson, a journeyman professional who looked a lot older than he was. Surely, this guy wouldn't be the scorer of the winning goal! Things failed to improve and Ricky was substituted. The sight of the distraught Argentinian walking slowly around the pitch and down the tunnel, obviously heartbroken, will never leave me. Spurs pushed forward and won a free kick on the edge of the area. Hoddle territory, but today nothing was going right and time was running out. As the ball left his boot, Hutchinson broke across the area, the ball clipped his shoulder and flew into the net. We erupted! I can remember my mate, Dean, leaping on me from the step above and the pair of us rolling down several more with dozens of fellow supporters. Extra time came and went with little incident and it would be a replay at Wembley for the first time in history.

Five days later we were back. I had returned in between to see England play Brazil, but all week my thoughts had been that we couldn't play that badly again. Outside the ground I got involved in a kickabout as Spurs and City fans passed the time away. For the rest of my life I would be able to say that I played football at Wembley on Cup Final day. Even George Best couldn't say that!

On the real pitch the teams served up a classic in one of the best finals ever. Saturday's desperate figure, Ricky Villa, wasted no time putting things right and opened the scoring early on. But as on Saturday, City wouldn't roll over and Steve Mackenzie hit a stunning equaliser. Worse followed as City took the lead from the penalty spot through Kevin Reeves. This certainly wasn't in the script! Three quarters of the crowd were behind Tottenham that night and as one we gave our all vocally. Our prayers were answered and Garth Crooks levelled.

Then, probably the best moment of my life! Tony Galvin broke down the left and released Ricky Villa again. Ricky ran and ran as blue shirts surrounded him. Pass it, pass it, pass it!! Still he kept twisting in and out of tackles. Steve Archibald was going mental yards away, unmarked with an open goal. Ricky kept going. PASS IT...GOOOAALLL!! The ball was in the net, Ricky was still running, but this was in celebration of one of the best goals the twin towers ever saw.

After what had seemed like an eternity the final whistle blew and the cup was ours!

"When Steve goes up to lift the FA Cup, we'll be there," we all sang. We were there and Steve Perryman was holding the cup proudly in our direction. Tears were streaming down my face and even now when I see that moment, I get goose bumps and feel emotional. I think all true supporters will understand that.

Now it was time to party! After the endless lap of honour we returned to the coach and opened the bottles of champagne that we had expectantly brought with us. Back to White Hart Lane and an all-night party outside the ground with the team's return being the highlight. The following morning I arrived back home on our local milk float. I swear that is true!

Wembley became a second home to me with Spurs in the next twelve months as we defended the FA Cup in a replay against QPR, lost to Liverpool in the Milk Cup and played Aston Villa and Liverpool in Charity Shield matches. Added to that were numerous England matches, but Wembley never lost its magic. Every visit brought excitement and a feeling of tradition. I was one of the lucky ones because I was there.

Admittedly, Wembley is a pig to get away from after the match, and the London Underground system struggles to cope with the crowd leaving at full time. The motorway network is not easy either and I have always felt for the fans leaving after a midweek England match with a journey back up north to follow.

Regardless, Wembley is the only place for our national stadium to be. There has to be a focal venue and, although the Midlands is more geographically located, the history is in North West

London. Your opinion will vary depending on your location probably, but the travelling circus of England's matches during the rebuilding of Wembley left me cold. I went to White Hart Lane to see England play Holland and felt detached from the experience. Remember this is a ground I love and have cherished memories at, but England playing there did not work for me.

Thankfully, new Wembley finally opened and the ground is remarkable. A little expensive to build, and a little late, but still stunning. The old stadium needed a revamp and it is a pity that the twin towers could not be incorporated in the new stadium, but you can't have everything.

One criticism, however, is the Centenary Club seating for the big wigs and corporate people. At every match we see a huge percentage of empty seats directly opposite the TV cameras as the occupants lap up the hospitality of the event. Why has nobody thought of switching the corporate seating to the other side of the pitch so viewers at home do not see a half empty area at a huge match? Is that too easy a solution to an embarrassing problem?

I attended the last big event at Wembley before the bulldozers moved in, a concert by Bon Jovi, and my memories were working overtime. I estimate around a hundred visits to matches at Wembley, club and country. I've celebrated the best day of my life there, I've cried there, I've lost there. I was there for Gazza's free kick on St. Hotspur Day when we beat Arsenal in the FA Cup Semi-Final and again when he pretty much destroyed his career a few weeks later in the final against Forest.

I was there when we, amazingly, lost to Coventry in the final and I was there for Live Aid and Wham's last concert. I was there when Keegan's England blew it and when Terry Venables nearly took us all the way in Euro 96. I was there when Lineker messed up the chance to equal Charlton's all-time scoring record and when Viv Anderson became England's first black player.

I wasn't there for the White Horse final, 1966, and all that, the Matthews final or the Hungarians teaching us a lesson. I wasn't there when the Jocks dug up the pitch or when an unknown Pole, labelled a clown, broke our hearts. I wasn't there when Bob Stokoe danced across the pitch or Charlie George lay down in celebration or when Keegan and Bremner got sent off for fighting.

Nor was I there when United beat Benfica to realise the dream of the Busby Babes, nor when Ajax conquered Europe with total football, but I remember them and all the others. They are part of my memories and if you are a football fan, you will remember them as well. They are part of history, the history of Wembley. The new ground will have its own memories in time.

I cannot imagine the national stadium being anywhere else.

CHAPTER 15 – THE GREATS
Magicians on a stage of grass

Elsewhere in this book I have covered my Tottenham heroes, but who were the best from outside White Hart Lane that I have seen?

As a team, I have to plump for the Liverpool side of the late seventies and early eighties. They were pretty much unstoppable. Dalglish, Souness, Keegan, McDermott, Hansen, Rush, Beardsley, Barnes…the list is endless and they always seemed to fit into the side as soon as they were signed or brought through the ranks.

They played with flair and pace. Kenny Dalglish was a magician and as good as any opponent I ever saw face Spurs.

Graeme Souness was as hard as nails and with Jimmy Case or Ray Kennedy alongside him, you had to be pretty good to get through their midfield. If you did, you found a defence as mean as any ever to have played the game. A goal against Liverpool was to be savoured.

I was at Anfield the day they hit Spurs for seven. It was the complete performance and, although finding our feet back in the top flight, we were not a poor side at all. Their seventh goal was one of the best moves I can recall. Dalglish found Case inside his own half. One touch then a forty yard ball to Heighway racing down the wing. First time to the far post and McDermott headed home. If you look at the goals on YouTube, Spurs could only be found completely at fault for one of them. Any team would have struggled to stop the rest. By the way, nobody remembers that Tottenham should have taken the lead that day, but wasted a chance when three on one with Ray Clemence. Maybe we upset them!

Liverpool ruled not only English football, but Europe as well, brushing anybody that got in their way to one side. They should have been the first English team to win the treble, but just missed out in the FA Cup Final in 1977 losing to Manchester United. Four days later they lifted the European Cup. That is the mark of a great side. The ability to bounce back after a major blow.

Manchester United's class of '92 were not that far behind in my opinion. Title after title after title was stacked up in the Old Trafford trophy room under Fergie. United were as dominant in this era as Liverpool had been previously, and probably should have won more in Europe. With the core of the team for an entire decade being the product of their youth system, the players added were a perfect fit.

Eric Cantona became their talisman during the early part of this success and, with the youngsters that Alan Hansen famously said 'would win nothing', destroyed the opposition. How could you fail to deliver with talent like Beckham, Scholes, the Nevilles, Schmeichel in goal, Roy Keane bossing the midfield and Cole, Yorke, Sheringham and Van Nistelrooy knocking them in? With Bruce and Pallister at the heart of the defence, strikers had their work cut out to make an impact.

Arsenal's invincibles deserve a mention. For several years they played some wonderful football. With the famous back four of Dixon, Winterburn, Adams and Bould in front of Seaman, they were never going to concede many goals. Viera was a beast in midfield with Pires, Overmars, Petit and Parlour buzzing around. Up top, Bergkamp and Henry, two of the absolute best to have played in our league.

Over the years, Forest were a bit special under Cloughie, so were Villa for a short period. Both won European Cups. Newcastle under Keegan were everybody's second favourite team with their 'you score three and we'll get four' attitude, but won nothing, and Leeds had their moments too until the club imploded..

In the last ten years Chelsea and Manchester City have hit the summit of our football. Chelsea have been in the best run of success in their history. The early seventies team was exciting, but lacked consistency. Recent Chelsea had a core of Cech, Terry, Lampard and Drogba which gave them that consistency. The only place that lacked consistency was the dug out with countless managers given the sack despite delivering in most cases. City play some great stuff, but cannot seem to adapt to Europe. Until they do, they will always fall short of the other sides I have mentioned.

From abroad I loved the Ajax and Bayern Munich sides of the seventies, followed a decade later by Gullit's Milan. More recently it has all been about Barcelona and Real Madrid and their array of superstars. Bayern are currently strong again too, but the Spanish sides have had that magic about them with Messi, Ronaldo and all the rest.

International sides that have impressed me over the years range from the Germans and Dutch of the seventies, Argentina from 1978, Spain in the recent past and, obviously, Brazil from 1970. I have covered World Cups elsewhere in this book, so I won't repeat my thoughts here.

On to individual players then. I cannot list all the greats I have seen in the flesh. I would need another twenty chapters to do that. What I can say is how lucky I have been to see such wonderful talent with my own eyes.

I'll start at world level. Everybody has an opinion on the best ever. For many it is Pele, but I go for Maradona. He almost single-handedly won the World Cup in 1986 with an unforgettable tournament. In 1990, he dragged a poor Argentina side to the final. He took Napoli to the Italian title for the only two occasions in their history. Maradona was simply unplayable. Kick him, and he got more determined. Play fairly against him, and you couldn't get near him. It is a shame that scandal and incidents away from the pitch cloud many people's opinion of him. Maybe in time Messi or Ronaldo will rival Maradona as the best ever, but I cannot see me changing my selection.

I struggled to decide how to select my best seen players in our league however. I finally decided to include only those that I saw face Tottenham with my own eyes and, as I have already picked a greatest Spurs team, I am not including any of the Tottenham players.

I took on an impossible Best Opposition Team selection challenge for two reasons. One, that it would really make me remember some great players and, secondly, I could mention more players that way. As soon as I started, I knew it was going to be impossible. There are too many! Nearly fifty years of watching football, well over a thousand matches seen live, and God only knows how many on the telly. How could I do this? It was bad enough picking my best-ever Spurs line up, but this was harder to do.

Then I found a solution. Well, sort of. I would pick two teams. A pre-Premiership team which would cover the first thirty years and a Premiership era team covering the last twenty years. It helped, but not much.

So, here we go with my Pre-Premiership team.

Peter Shilton in goal. Easy choice.

I have gone for three at the back, mainly to fit in more midfielders, but I have laced my choice with balance. Anyway, my three are Bobby Moore, Alan Hansen and Stuart Pearce. Two great ball players with the ability to read the game better than most and an absolute warrior. Get past them if you can!

Two midfielders who would have to be a bit defence-minded are next and Graeme Souness just had to be in this team. Alongside him, Bryan Robson. I feel people have forgotten just how good he was, as he rarely gets mentioned these days.

Those two would have to sit back a little bit to accommodate George Best, Bobby Charlton and Alan Ball, although Bally covered every blade of grass in every game, so could rotate with the other two.

Finally, up front Dalglish was the first name on the sheet and Ian Rush was impossible to leave out for his amazing strike rate alone.

There were so many legends that I have had to leave out. Law,

Bremner, Bell, Butcher, McDermott, Sansom to name a few.

The Premiership era team was harder!

Scmeichel in goal was simple. Nobody else came close.

Tony Adams, John Terry and Nemanja Vidic as a defensive three.

Patrick Viera and Roy Keane as defensive midfielders, providing they didn't start on each other!

That allows me five attack-minded players, so Zola and Cantona playing wide with a licence to cut inside seems like a start.

Bergkamp in the hole with Shearer and Henry up front.

No place for Ronaldo, Van Nistelrooy, Gerrard, Lampard, Rio, Scholes. How can I leave them out? I can't fit them in either though.

I know there are no full backs, or wing backs in either team. I expect the back three and defensive midfielders to deal with that problem. This was about fitting in the legends as I saw it and not picking balanced teams. One thing is for sure though; I would have loved to see the midfield battle between Viera and Keane against Souness and Robson. What a mouth-watering thought!

I always knew how fortunate I had been to see so many greats play live, but writing this chapter has made me realise that I was honoured to have seen so many legends.

CHAPTER 16 – SKY TV
Into the twenty-first century

Once upon a time BBC and ITV ruled our screens. A meagre hour a week of highlights was all we got to see with, occasionally, a bonus game on *Sportsnight* in midweek!

Now we can watch every kick of so many games it is unreal. The games not shown live are given extended highlights programmes and the fan is the winner with twenty-four hour a day football!

From the days in the late eighties when satellite TV was in its infancy we could not have seen this coming. The master stroke was when the Premiership TV rights were snapped up by Sky. All of a sudden the company had a product to push, and boy have they pushed it!

From the very start Sky went over the top with cheerleaders and firework displays at their chosen matches. With the exception of the lady at Wolves who stopped a stray rocket in the face, fans loved the added glamour and glitz. But Sky was not only about razzmatazz and has evolved into a superb medium for sports in general, not just football.

Let's start with a live match. With around an hour of pre-match chat there is never a stone left unturned. The content is top drawer and all the key people involved in the match are spoken to or a piece recorded on them. At the helm Jamie Redknapp, Jamie Carragher and Gary Neville are better than anybody who has gone before them. Originally, Andy Gray and Richard Keys previously pioneered technology, until they fell foul of the PC brigade. Add Martin Tyler as commentator and it is hard to see where the coverage could be improved.

With dozens of cameras in place, nothing is missed during a match and the speed that an incident can be shown again makes you wonder why FIFA still will not allow technology to help the officials, although they have finally relented to goal line technology, so who knows? It may be coming, but don't hold your breath! If you don't want to listen to Tyler and Neville, you could listen to two fans of the clubs on the Fanzone option! Admittedly, this can be a bit monotonous, but at times hilarious! What a great idea!

After the match both managers and key players are interviewed before moving on to Neville, Redknapp and Carragher's gadgets! The technology they have at their fingertips is pretty impressive. No moving Subbuteo players around here to emphasise a point!

The match choice is incredible. Most weekends have three or four live Premiership matches plus a handful of Scottish and Spanish matches as well. Add a splattering of League football and everybody is catered for. *Football First* gives you the opportunity to watch any of the day's matches from the Premiership later that day.

Champions League nights give a choice of every game being played that night. Unbelievable! When I was younger the thought of being able to choose between any game from eight never entered my mind.

Recently in the same week I watched live the following matches, Tottenham v Arsenal, Villa v Wolves, Leeds v Millwall, Inter v Barcelona, Lyon v Bayern and the Manchester derby. What a week!

Saturday viewing is as good as it gets. Start the day with three hours of the terrific Helen on *Soccer AM*, although not the same since Tim left, before *Soccer Saturday*! Whoever came up with this format is a genius!

Four ex-players watching matches on monitors and telling us what is happening. It should not work, but it does big time! Jeff Stelling hosting is brilliant. Passionate about the game and infectious, he keeps the seriously long programme impossible to walk away from. The guests are outspoken and behave as if it was a group of fans watching. With initial names like George Best and

Rodney Marsh through to Paul Merson, Charlie Nicholas, Phil Thompson and Matt Le Tissier currently, the mix has worked like a dream. In the same programme, going live to an ex-player at a ground adds to the quality, and Chris Kamara has to be the funniest football pundit ever! From laughing uncontrollably to not realising a player has been sent off, this format should not work. Again, it does!

Away from the actual matches the quality of the other programmes is equally strong. Twenty-four hours a day Sports News keeps you from missing anything. Programmes like *Sunday Supplement* that involve journalists talking about the recent stories are ground-breaking shows. The information gleaned from these shows replaces the need for a newspaper. Even in the close season there is always football to watch!

It is hard to find a negative comment and all that I can criticize is the extraordinary amount of money that Sky has pumped into the game playing a huge part in taking the game away from the man in the street. On the other hand, Sky has brought an unbelievable amount of football into our homes.

The Sky is the limit they say! It is difficult to see how football could be better covered than by Sky!

CHAPTER 17 – OFFICIALDOM
The blind leading the blind?

Let me get this clear. Decisions have to be made at every level in football. From the kit man upwards! Just as in so many industries, however, the higher up the ladder you go the more detached people become. Decisions get made that affect everybody apart from the person making it in the first place.

The Football Association have a duty to protect our game. In reality they are weak when they need to be strong and when common sense is required they come down with a sledgehammer.

'Evragate' is a good example of going over the top with a punishment. After the warm down incident between Chelsea ground staff and Manchester United players at Stamford Bridge, the FA had to act. I believe they got it wrong on a number of levels. Firstly, the punishment took too long to be decided, four months into the following season. Then a four match ban! Now, Evra clearly did something wrong, but he did not do everything that day and the rest were innocents. Surely, a match or two would have been sufficient.

But worst of all, why publish the whole transcript of the hearing on their official website? All they have done by doing that is set a precedent for future cases. Wait and see managers demanding to see the transcripts of other clubs hearings! Lunacy, and all of their own doing.

For decades the FA has consisted of faceless wonders dictating to the rest of football. In the last few seasons they have at least had the sense to bring in proper football people, such as Trevor Brooking, to assist. At least with proper football people involved we have half a chance of getting it right.

Unfortunately, we still have idiots there also. The recent

lobbying for an extra match to be fitted into the Premiership season is, in my opinion, ludicrous. The idea is to send all our teams to Timbuktoo or somewhere so that foreign followers of our game get the chance to see our stars. This is wrong on so many levels and really angers me. What about the loyal supporters in this country who attend matches week in, and week out, but could not get to Hong Kong or wherever?

Firstly, it is the English League and should be played in England. Having an odd number of matches would also bring unfair fixtures in some cases. Some teams would end up facing Manchester United three times in the league while somebody would get three cracks at Sunderland. Who would decide the fixtures and how to ensure fair play?

Obviously the reason for this is money. Here is my solution. Leave the league fixtures alone. Organise a pre-season competition that all Premiership sides had to compete in abroad, a bit like a mini World Cup. Foreign countries see our players at first hand, the FA get their wedge and the players get match fit. Win, win, win! So easy it hurts!

Inconsistency at the FA is another area which causes me concern. I can recall Rio Ferdinand receiving a four match ban for elbowing an opponent. No problem with that, but two weeks later Steven Gerrard did exactly the same thing and had no punishment. How about a neutral panel to assess these things, made up of ex-players, ex-managers and maybe a journalist or fan to give a true balance?

Last moan at the FA, mainly because they do not deserve any more space, is their ability to give the England managers job to the wrong man so consistently over the years. I cover this in detail elsewhere in the book, but Greenwood, Taylor and, worst of all, McClaren? Why?

Also, in my opinion, the England manager should be English! Sorry Sven and Fabio.

Incredibly, there are worse organisations in football than the FA; FIFA and UEFA! The rulers of world and European football. With the top two men at the table for so many years, Sepp Blatter and Michele Platini, we would have been better off with Laurel and Hardy!

Both of these seem to hate the English and I always felt we would never have parity with the rest of the world while they were in place. Any opportunity to have a dig at us was taken and it has been delightful to see how annoyed they were at English domination in Europe in recent seasons! Now, if only we can win the World Cup…

FIFA's constant dismissal regarding the use of goal line technology was a joke. Too many times teams were cheated out of goals which had been missed by match officials. It could be about the time it would take to check a monitor because Gary Neville and co knew within seconds from his Sky TV seat! We no longer play in the dark ages and we need to catch up with rugby and tennis to use technology to get it right.

Three incidents out of countless ones I can recall, highlighted the need for this to happen. Tottenham's 'goal' at Old Trafford which was about three feet over the line and not seen by the lino who didn't go to Specsavers!

Birmingham's similar 'goal' at Portsmouth that denied them a cup semi-final for the first time in thirty years. Thierry Henry's blatant double handball that sent France to the World Cup instead of the Republic of Ireland!

Would Platini have a different view if it had been Robbie Keane playing basketball that night?

With the scandal that rocked football and tore FIFA apart, at least we are now rid of both Blatter and Platini. Neither went quietly and the governing bodies will do well to recover dignity in the short term. With court cases still to come it may never return.

Lastly on officials, the much maligned referee. Okay, the ref has a job to do and the best ref is the one you cannot remember at the end of the game. In recent years, 'celebrity' refs have turned up for matches appearing to desire to be the focal point of the match.

I have not got a problem with a genuine mistake being made by a ref. Technology would help, but without it we have to carry on. Where I have a problem is when the referee's assistant fails to assist and the role of the fourth official. What does he do other than monitor the injury time board and substitutions? He is on a radio to the ref so why can he not assist with the big calls? In an ideal world it would be his job to watch a TV monitor to ensure we got the correct decision.

I get infuriated when the ref bottles a decision. A foul that would be given ten times out of ten outside the penalty area is still a foul when it is inside the area, but so many times not given. Why?

Also, when there has been a controversial decision during a match, why should the ref not have to explain why he has given that decision after the game? Managers are forced into facing the TV cameras within minutes of the match ending, why not the ref?

CHAPTER 18 – MONEY
It's a rich man's world

'Money makes the world go around', so says the song! Tell that to Portsmouth fans! FA Cup winners in 2008, spent like crazy for a year and bust in 2010.

For several seasons it has been a question of when a top flight club goes bust. Pompey drew the short straw, but will not be the last if the craziness continues. Previously, Leeds went desperately close to folding, but the fire sale of all their players saved them from closure at the cost of dropping into the third tier of English football.

Portsmouth have had to sell their players also, but ended up with schoolboys on the bench as they couldn't fill the teamsheet. Where it will end for them is anybody's guess. Part of their problem has been boardroom unrest. Many clubs have suffered as people, with too much money and time on their hands, play with the emotions of everybody connected with a football club.

Portsmouth have had too many owners in too short a space of time. Other clubs have just been a rich man's plaything (Liverpool and Newcastle spring to mind) or run by a misguided fan at the helm (Tottenham and Leeds).

Liverpool were in no man's land for a while, with two American owners who reportedly, didn't speak to each other. That has not helped the club in their efforts to get back to where they are competing for the title on a regular basis. A few years ago I said Liverpool would never win the title with Rafa Benitez in charge and the background chaos. The stability they now appear to have with no dramas off the pitch will give Jurgen Klopp the chance to challenge.

Foreign owners are still in the relatively early days in our game and I wonder about the motives when one of our clubs is snapped up. Manchester City is the obvious and most worrying club as money is no object for their Arab owner. City have been propelled much quicker than any other club in history to football's elite. They have been a bit of a joke for years as managers came and went quicker than Linford Christie running for a bus. Then the money arrived, a whole new team appeared, the manager, who was doing a good job, got sacked and the club expects the Premiership title to follow annually.

Randy Lerner, at Aston Villa, started in a good way. He kept out of the limelight and things looked good for the club, but he lost interest, stopped funding and started sacking managers left, right and centre. Villa are down in the Championship and Lerner is off into the sunset.

The Roman empire at Chelsea has also calmed down after the initial circus. The Russian has also sat back since he got rid of Jose Mourinho and, I can honestly say, I do not think I have ever heard him speak!

While I am wary of foreign investment there have been some disasters at the hands of English owners too. Peter Ridsdale at Leeds and Mike Ashby at Newcastle are classic examples of how not to run football clubs, for very different reasons. Ridsdale got caught up in the glory and spent money the club did not have and more!

There is a story, I am reliably told, of one incident involving Ridsdale during the boom days at Elland Road. A player went in for contract negotiations with his agent with the Leeds chairman. Before going in the agent told the player he was aiming for twenty grand a week. When they walked in Ridsdale got straight to the point. "Forty grand a week is the offer," he announced!

"Forty grand?" said the delighted agent.

But before he could accept the offer Ridsdale countered with, "Okay fifty grand and that's my final offer!"

I hope with all my heart that story is true!

Ridsdale's leadership of Leeds was masked for a while as the team was performing well and big names were at the club. The trial of Bowyer and Woodgate took the headlines for several months also and then O'Leary's book, *Leeds United on Trial*, deflected the attention. Ridsdale survived for longer than he should have done and more damage to the club occurred.

After he left the club fighting for survival he turned up a while later as chairman of Cardiff. Cardiff were quickly fighting for financial survival. Has nothing been learnt? That is the mess that led them to red shirts and an Asian owner who boos his own team!

Ashby is a different kind of threat to our clubs. In my opinion, he has more in common with Del Boy than a true football chairman and has single-handedly destroyed Newcastle. From sitting with the fans with his barcode shirt on, to appointing Dennis Wise as Director of Football, everything he has done has been wrong. Even the desperate appointment of Alan Shearer, when the club was all but down, was an attempt to deflect attention I believe. Shearer failed and left as quickly as he got there.

The only good thing he has done has been to appoint Chris Hughton and Rafa Benitez to the hot seat. Hughton did a good job and returned the Geordies to the top flight at the first attempt, but then got sacked the following season. Rafa came in too late to save the club from relegation and now he is staying for the push to come back, Newcastle have a chance of making things right. Hopefully, for the Toon Army, Ashby can soon get a better price for the club and get out leaving a better owner in place. Anyone who wants to rename St. James' Park shouldn't be there in the first place!

Of course, the owners are not the only problem with our footballing finances. Players earn too much! I have said elsewhere in this book that I do not begrudge them earning what they can, but certain things are just not right!

Ashley Cole's claims that he nearly crashed his car upon hearing that Arsenal were only offering to put his wage up to fifty five grand a week is one of them. Cole is a decent player; nowhere near as good as he thinks he is, but decent nonetheless. The following saga about if he stayed or went to Chelsea was embarrassing for all involved. Cole eventually got his move and the money he craved. His dignity did not make the move to Stamford Bridge though!

Cole was probably pushed into contract talks and, ultimately, a transfer by an agent lurking In the background. Agents are the single biggest threat to our game. In some cases, they manipulate content players into asking for a pay rise or transfer and then creaming off a huge wedge for themselves. The more a player moves club the more money the agent makes also. That money leaves the game. Why do we need agents at all? There is nothing wrong in a player taking advice from somebody during contract negotiations but, in some cases, the agent does the deal and then tells the player after the event! By then the wheels are in motion and the player is moving regardless of if he wants to or not. Ask Carlos Tevez!

Agents have played a huge part in driving up transfer fees also. This has led to many clubs being priced out of being able to keep their star players. West Ham, for example, have become a feeder club in recent years for their rivals. Lampard, Defoe, Carrick, Cole, Johnson and Ferdinand are all current England internationals who have departed Upton Park after coming through the academy. What a team they could have had if they had kept these and others who have left. Instead, they floundered around fighting for survival most seasons.

Even the big boys struggle to keep their stars. Ronaldo finally left Manchester United for Real Madrid after a couple of years of 'will he stay, will he go?' stories. Even the £80 million pound fee does not fill the void left at Old Trafford! Henry and Viera eventually left Arsenal in pretty much the same way. Spurs couldn't hold on to Bale and Torres left Liverpool.

Money does make the world go round. The question is, 'what happens to our game when it runs out?'

CHAPTER 19 – CONCLUSION
Time added on

I've made it to the final chapter. Hopefully, you are still with me and my memories and opinions have stirred some of your own.

I want to make it clear that I have tried to be unbiased in all of my opinions, but I wear my heart on my sleeve and I bleed blue and white, so at times I may have failed to be neutral. Sorry Arsenal!

Hopefully, my passion for football has shone through in this book. From my limited playing days, to my management in youth football and the decades of following one of the giants of English football, the game has meant the world to me. It still does, but I do not see me racing down the wing anytime soon!

In many ways it has changed for the better, but in many ways I believe that we have lost something special, mainly due to the commercialism of today's game. Do the kids of today feel it like my generation did? I don't think so. We played in the street until we couldn't see the ball and I would go indoors raving about the goal that I had scored that went in off the lamppost. If we were not kicking a ball around, we were off on our bikes, playing tennis, swimming or something else that involved sport.

I was lucky that my school gave me such a wide variety of sporting choices. We played almost every sport you can think of, even handball. We were allowed to box, unlike today where the Health and Safety muppets would put a stop to that in an instant.

Today, it seems technology means much more than actually moving around. So many kids sit in front of a computer trying to car jack or shoot somebody in a game. It's a real shame because some of them will never have experiences like I did as a youngster.

I can still remember organising a match with friends from school and producing a programme for this event. A one off game with the obligatory jumpers for goalposts on the Satellite, a field near to where we lived. I remember we drew 3-3 and we had called our team Zodiac FC. I would have been about ten-years-old at the time.

In four decades time, will today's youth remember with a smile, the day they did well on Grand Theft Auto? Unlikely!

The more serious reality to the technological threat is that kids have no need to go out and run around. If that is the case, where are tomorrow's players and supporters going to come from?

West Ham have grabbed the initiative with their move to the Olympic Stadium, where £99 will buy a season ticket for a child. This is a really good thing and should be adopted by all top flight clubs. Overpricing of matches will kill the game if we are not careful.

A friend of mine went to see Torquay play last season in the conference. It cost him £16 to get in! I would want to be playing if I had paid that much for a non-league game. I understand that lower level clubs need to make as much money as possible, but if prices were more realistic, would the attendance not be higher and the fan base more solid?

Sky TV continues to plough bucket loads of cash into the game and, this season, the Premiership clubs are receiving a reported £100 million windfall. What will they do with that money? Higher transfer fees and wages almost certainly. Surely, ticket prices need to be subsidised in some way?

Commercial activities ensure even more bucket loads of cash so, if invested wisely, the clubs can reduce the price at the gate. For every corporate guest who is there for a one day jolly, there are a hundred true fans who have been priced out of the game.

The season ahead will be interesting.

England are looking for a new manager following the scandal surrounding Big Sam.

Leicester are defending their title and competing in the

Champions League.

Spurs have a team capable of challenging for the title again.

Mourinho and Guardiola are starting life in Manchester, Klopp is starting his first full season at Anfield. Conte starts at Chelsea and Koeman at Goodison Park. Hull, Burnley and Middlesbrough are back and will be scrapping to stay in the top flight. Rafa will be trying to get the Toon Army back up and Rangers are back in Scotland. Zlatan has arrived at United.

West Ham have a new home and Spurs are starting their last season at the Lane. That will be emotional and I don't want to think about it just yet.

This will be the first season without Blatter and Platini running FIFA and UEFA. Hopefully, there will be a culture change there, but the legal and criminal prosecutions will rumble on for ages to come.

Finally, my hopes for our game are simple. More money into grass roots football is needed. Maybe 1% of all transfer fees would be a starting point? Failing that, where does the money go from FA fines imposed when a manager speaks out of turn? Let's use some of that.

Honesty in the game would be nice. Less waving an imaginary card, less rolling around, less diving, less conning the referee and less all-in wrestling in the box at every corner.

Referees explaining decisions after the game.

More use of the technology available for the really important calls.

Common sense prevailing and the World Cup being taken away from Quatar in 2022.

An England team that does well at a tournament.

A Tottenham title win.

Kenneth Wolstenholme once said, "They think it's all over, it is now."

It is, and I hope you enjoyed reading it as much as I did reliving it.

The Author

Paul Buck was born in London, but has lived in Devon for the last nine years.

He lives with his partner, surrounded by hundreds of football books. He is a Tottenham Hotspur fan and has two grown-up children, of which one is an Arsenal fan!

Following careers in the print trade and financial credit industry, he now runs his own football programme and memorabilia business. This is his first published book.

www.apexpublishing.co.uk